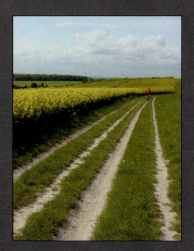

mountain bike rides
in & around
Wiltshire & Dorset

ROUGH RIDE GUIDE

All rights reserved ©. No part of this book may be reproduced, stored in any retrieval systems or transmitted in any form or by any means, electronic, mechanical, photocopy, recording or otherwise without the express permission of the publishers and copyright owner.

To the best of the publisher's knowledge the information in this book was correct at the time of press.

No responsibility can be accepted for the error or their consequences. Text and compilation copyright © owned by Rough Ride Guide Ltd 2007

Feedback: If you know of any information on changes of access rights, information etc or would like to recommend a good route, please contact us at info@roughrideguide.co.uk and will endeavour to reward your efforts.

First published in 2007 by:

Rough Ride Guide Ltd
Walnut Tree Offices
The Old Road
Pishill
Henley-on-Thames
Oxon
RG9 6HS

ISBN 978-0-9548829-5-2

Printed by
Stephens & George Print Group
in the UK

The maps in this book have been reproduced by permission of Ordnance Survey on behalf of the Controller of Her Majesty's Stationery Office, © Crown Copyright 100037674.

DISCLAIMER

Mountain biking is a dangerous and addictive sport. The authors and publishers take no responsibility for accident, injury, death, loss of friends, or inconvenience sustained by any user of this guide as a result of information or advice contained within this guide.

This book provides information on routes with a personal insight, but is not necessarily proof of the existence of a right of way, and does not guarantee the safety and well being of any user using the information or advice contained in this guide.

Ride safely, within your limits and wear a helmet. RRG accepts no responsibility for any breakage to you or your bike, getting lost, injured, tired, lost, hungry, wet, grumpy, sunburnt, cold, or lost.

mountain bike rides in & around Wiltshire & Dorset

SPECIAL THANKS TO:

My wife Sarah who has inspired and supported me throughout this project.

My friends & family for their help and support.

The riders, clubs and bike shops who have showed us their favourite trails.

Ken Williams for reasearch and technical advice.

You for buying this book, I hope you have some great rides and adventures.

EDITORS
Max Darkins
Richard Sanders

DESIGNERS
Kate Lester
Lee Bainbrigge

PHOTOGRAPHS
Max Darkins
Richard Sanders
Sarah Darkins
Ken Williams
Specialized

foreword by the author

Since the release of the first A4 Rough Ride Guide books we've been lucky to have received lots of really positive feedback from riders. It also made us aware of the need for a smaller, cheaper version of the book - same concept and quality, but not such a big cash outlay. With the option to 'mix n match' further sections into your book through our website, we feel that we have come up with a truly unique product that we hope you enjoy using as much as we did making it.

Wiltshire & Dorset is not always thought of as a mountain biking hot spot, but it has lots of lush green, rolling countryside, with plenty of off-road riding, thanks to the number of bridleways around. Salisbury Plain is also a hot spot for military activity, and while they provide some explosive entertainment, and sightings of tanks, etc, they also look after the land very well, meaning some tracks will still be ok to ride in the wet winter months. There are also lots of good local ales to sample, while out on these rides.

In these A5 guidebooks we've tried to provide information on nearby train stations and how to get to the start of the ride. If trains really aren't feasible, try to share lifts, its far more sociable and an easy way to reduce your collective carbon footprint.

Whether you're simply searching for more local rides or are using this book as a guide on your holiday, I hope that you have some great rides and new experiences, and don't stop telling us what you think.

We have a 'notice board' on our website which we will use to provide up-to-date news and information on the routes e.g. conditions, changes, etc. The success of this 'notice board' will rely heavily on your input, so please e-mail us with any news and information you have.

Mountain bikers are generally a friendly bunch, who will stop and chat, admire each others bikes and assist with breakdowns, so lets keep it that way. It is a sport that anyone can enjoy, so make the effort to make everyone feel welcome, whatever their age, sex or ability.

Happy riding.

Max Darkins

INTRODUCTION

The Rough Ride Guide books are designed to let *you* choose which sections you would like to have in your book. The standard book has a selection of routes, to which you can add more routes and further supplements, such as our maintenance & repair manual. These can all be purchased from our website www.roughrideguide.co.uk.

TOP TIP: We advice all riders, especially new comers to the sport, to get the 'Introduction to mountain biking' as it has lots of useful information and tips, to enable you to get and make the most of the sport, and gain maximum enjoyment.

THE ROUTE GRADING

Please bear in mind that peoples opinions vary, as well as their speed and line choice, which all play a big factor in determining the difficulty level of a route. Grading our routes is also made more difficult by the fact that our routes usually have shortcut and extension options, which is why our routes usually have a grading between 2 levels.

We have graded our the routes from Easy to Extreme, bearing in mind the terrain, distance, height gained, and opportunity to bail-out, or be rescued should naything go wrong.

Also, to keep some consistency and familiarity to grading trails, we have adopted the ratings and colour coding used by various parties, including the Forestry Commission (but our yellow is their green).

EASY (YELLOW): Suitable for beginners. Generally wide, well surfaced, easy going tracks.

MEDIUM (BLUE): Suitable for intermediate riders. Rougher terrain, single track, requires a choice of line and some technical ability.

HARD (RED): Suitable for experienced riders only. Good bike control required, quick decision making, and some healthy lungs.

EXTREME (BLACK): Suitable for very experienced and competent riders. Contains some very technical and potentially dangerous terrain.

COUNTRYSIDE CODE

Only ride on open trails
Be in control of your bike at all times
Slow down or stop and let people pass by
Warn people of your presence by calling or ringing a bell, pass slowly and be polite
Don't scare any animals
Don't leave any rubbish
Look ahead and be aware
Be kind & courteous to other trail users
Shut gates behind you

TOP TIP: Fix a bell to your bike to politely warn others of your presence - it has even been known to raise a smile from walkers.

BLOCKED TRAILS

There are a couple of very useful websites provided by the CTC that enable you to report / enter the details of a blocked Right of Way e.g. a locked gate at www.clearthattrail.org.uk or for pot holes in roads (a big cause of cycling accidents) at www.fillthathole.org.uk.

- **NOTE:** You are perfectly within your rights to continue along the path (or where it should be), by passing around or climbing over the obstacle.

- **NOTE:** If an aggressive animal e.g. a dog is stopping you from progressing on a public ROW, inform the police.

USING ROUGH RIDE GUIDE MAPS

Our aim when producing these guidebooks has been to offer clear, fun and challenging routes, suitable for all abilities. To achieve this we have used the best mapping, sought local riders knowledge, and provided shortcut and extension options. This will ensure that everyone can find and ride the best trails, with minimum effort and hassle.

■ **NOTE:** We have made every effort to ensure that these routes only use legal paths, but access rights can change or mistakes be made, so if you are ever unsure, please walk your bike to avoid confrontation.

(RRG) ABBREVIATIONS

To reduce the amount of text you have to read through, we have abbreviated the frequently used words. It looks a long list, but most are obvious.

L = Left
R = Right
SA = Straight ahead / across
Bear = A bend of less than 90 degrees
T-J = T-Junction (usually at 180 degrees)
Fork = Track splits into two directions
X-rds = Cross roads (4 road junction)
X-tracks = As X-rds, but tracks not roads
DH = Downhill
UH = Uphill
FP = Footpath
BW = Bridleway
ByW = By-Way
(P)ROW = (Public) Right of way
RUPP = Road used as public path
BOAT = By-way open to all traffic
DT = Double track (wide enough for a car)
ST = Single track (narrow trail).

■ **NOTE:** Emboldened directions provide the 'must know' information, and the other directions provide greater detail for when you may be unsure.

DISTANCE

The (blue) main route is usually around 30 kilometres / 20 miles, which will be suitable for most competent and fit mountain bikers, with (yellow) shortcut and (red) extension options for riders wanting to adjust the length to suit their needs.

HEIGHT

The main route shows the distance and amount of climbing. The extension or shortcut will have a + or - figure, to show the change in distance and climbing from the main route. For example, if the main route is 30 kilometres with 500 metres of climbing, and you ride this and the extension which reads +7 kilometress and +150 meters of climbing, you will ride a total of 37 kilometres with 650 metres of climbing.

TOP TIP: A bike computer is very useful to show you exactly how far you have gone, so you can follow the distances we provide between points. Discrepancies do occur, so use them as a guide, not gospel.

■ **NOTE:** The amount of climbing involved on the route is just as important as the distance. Generally, 300+ meters of climbing over 15 kilometres is strenuous, so any ride of 45 kilometres and over 900 meters of climbing is going to be very tough. See the route profile below.

We have provided distances in both kilometres, and miles (in brackets), as although we are starting to become familiar with KM, most of us have grown up using and thinking in miles.

ROUTE PROFILE

These are at the bottom of the route directions, showing you the cross section / height gained and lost, on the main route. The numbers above the profile correlate to the route text numbering.

ORDNANCE SURVEY (LANDRANGER) MAP KEY

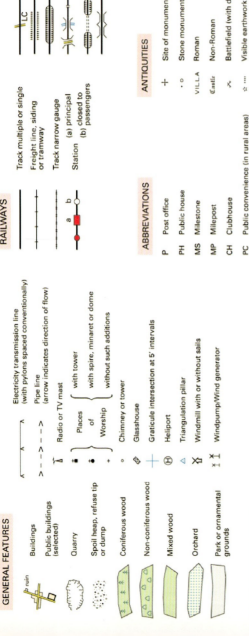

ORDNANCE SURVEY (LANDRANGER) MAP KEY

ROADS AND PATHS   Not necessarily rights of way

- Service area
- Junction number
- M1
- Elevated
- Unfenced
- Footbridge
- A 470 (T)
- Dual carriageway
- A 493
- B 4518
- A 855   B 885
- Bridge
- Ferry P   Ferry V

- Motorway (dual carriageway)
- Motorway under construction
- Trunk road
- Main road
- Main road under construction
- Secondary road
- Narrow road with passing places
- Road generally more than 4 m wide
- Road generally less than 4 m wide
- Other road, drive or track
- Path
- Gradient: steeper than 20% (1 in 5)
  14% to 20% (1 in 7 to 1 in 5)
- Gates   Road Tunnel
- Ferry (passenger)   Ferry (vehicle)

PUBLIC RIGHTS OF WAY

- Footpath
- Bridleway
- Road used as public path
- Byway open to all traffic

Public rights of way shown on this map have been taken from local authority definitive maps and later amendments. The map includes changes notified to Ordnance Survey by (date). The symbols show the defined route so far as the scale of mapping will allow.
Rights of way are not shown on maps of Scotland.

Rights of way are liable to change and may not be clearly defined on the ground. Please check with the relevant local authority for the latest information.

The representation on this map of any other road, track or path is no evidence of the existence of a right of way.

Danger Area   Firing and Test Ranges in the area.
Danger! Observe warning notices

OTHER PUBLIC ACCESS

- · · · Other route with public access

The exact nature of the rights on these routes and the existence of any restrictions may be checked with the local highway authority. Alignments are based on the best information available. These routes are not shown on maps of Scotland.

- ♦ National Trail, Long Distance Route, selected Recreational Paths
- ● National/Regional Cycle Network
- — Surfaced cycle route
- 4 National Cycle Network number
- 8 Regional Cycle Network number

ROCK FEATURES

outcrop   cliff   scree

HEIGHTS

- 50   Contours are at 10 metres vertical interval
- · 144 Heights are to the nearest metre above mean sea level

Heights shown close to a triangulation pillar refer to the station height at ground level and not necessarily to the summit.

1 metre = 3.2808 feet

TOURIST INFORMATION

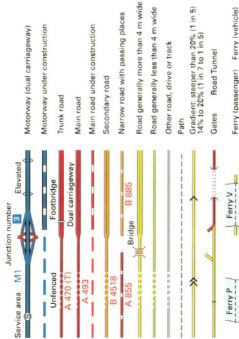

- Information centre, all year/seasonal
- Selected places of tourist interest
- Viewpoint
- Parking
- Youth hostel
- Golf course or links
- Bus or coach station
- Picnic site
- Camp site
- Caravan site
- Public telephone
- Motoring organisation telephone
- Public convenience (in rural areas) PC

ROUTES

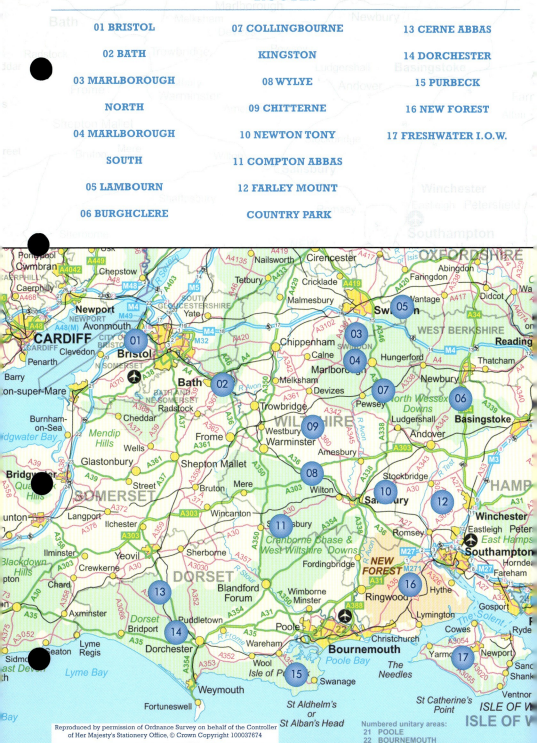

No	NAME	GRADING	DISTANCE (KM)	+ / - (KM)	CLIMBING (METRES)
01	BRISTOL	MEDIUM / HARD	28.2	-16.7	570
02	BATH	MEDIUM / HARD	29.5	-4.6	640
03	MARLBOROUGH NORTH	EASY / MEDIUM	25	-7.25	400
04	MARLBOROUGH SOUTH	MEDIUM	24.1	-5.2 & -6.6	380
05	LAMBOURN	MEDIUM	34.6	-9.2	490
06	BURGHCLERE	MEDIUM / HARD	27.4	+17.2	490
07	COLLINGBOURNE KINGSTON	MEDIUM	22.8	+6.5	450
08	WYLYE	EASY / MEDIUM	26	-8.4	425
09	CHITTERNE	MEDIUM	32.5	-11.3 OR +10.9	400
10	NEWTON TONY	MEDIUM	37.2	-	560
11	COMPTON ABBAS	MEDIUM / HARD	29.6	-8 & -6.3 OR +9.5	760
12	FARLEY MOUNT COUNTRY PARK	EASY / MEDIUM	42.2	-24	475
13	CERNE ABBAS	MEDIUM / HARD	28.7	-6.6 & -6 OR +8.2 & +7.1	590
14	DORCHESTER	EASY / MEDIUM	23.8	+6.3	460
15	PURBECK	MEDIUM / HARD	29.5	-7.4 OR +12	820
16	NEW FOREST	EASY / MEDIUM	VARIOUS	VARIOUS	NOT MUCH
17	FRESHWATER I.O.W.	MEDIUM / HARD	37	+7.25 OR -18.8	870

ROUTE INFORMATION

Leigh woods, Ashton Court, etc have lots & lots of superb technical single track (well) hidden within them. This route uses the Timberland Trail to help navigate and guarantee some great riding, but you need the help of a local to explore other tracks with any success. Nightmare when wet - avoid!

This route goes out the back of the University, and across a golf course, with great views. A good descent, takes you to a good fast section along the Avon Canal, before a very rocky, technical descent on Pipehouse lane. Then its another cycletrack, and a short descent, before a big climb back up to Bath. This ride works well in the wet.

Mostly double track, which gets more technical the faster you go, make it suitable for all abilities. Gets slippery when wet, and the 4x4's can churn up the trail where it hasn't been surfaced.

This route is very similar to the northern route, but a bit harder. There are shortcut options though, and navigation is easy, so the going is quick. Do both rides together for 1 hard loop. Slippery when wet.

This ride is very easy to navigate, with a long section along the the Ridgeway, which enables you to cover a lot of ground quickly. There is a shortcut option, and other escape routes, back downhill to the start if needed. Its nearly all along good double track, which can be hard going and slippery when wet.

The rutted double track of the Ridgeway basically provides a choice of single track trails, some of which work out well, others into deep pedal catching ruts - its all part of the fun as you race your mates. The 2nd part of the ride uses some nice quiet bridleways and country lanes, before steep downhill to finish.

Using some nice wide chalk tracks across the open rolling countryside, with some stiff climbs and descents. There is also some nice single track inside Collingbourne Woods, which the extension takes you along, but it is also worth exploring further. Hard going in wet conditions.

This route is pretty easy to navigate and has a useful shortcut, isn't too hilly and uses mostly good fire road tracks, which make it suitable for less experienced riders. The trails are fairly weather proof and fast going, but some sections will still get muddy and can get churned up.

This is quite typical riding for the Salisbury Plains, with good long tracks crossing the barren countryside. This is an active military area, and you pass right by the 'German village' (now probably a mock Bosnian village). Works pretty well in the (not severe) wet and gets more technical the faster you ride.

A very easy route to navigate, which drains well, making it an ideal winter ride. There are no big climbs or descents to face, but then there are no real shortcuts to it either. Most of the ride uses wide, well defined tracks, but there is some single track and a rocky climb in to keep things entertaining.

This is a fairly tough route, but there are some good shortcut options available. It is a hilly area, with some challenging climbs and descents, with dramatic views of this lovely countryside (where people like Madonna and Sting choose to live). The mud sticks well here, so avoid it in the wet.

Quite a long ride, but there isn't too much climbing involved, and the navigation is easy, so you should make good time. There is a shortcut option, or you could ride from King's Somborne to West Down (pub stop) and ride back again. Its not too technical, but still has some good trails and works well in the wet.

This route is very adaptable with all the shortcuts and extensions. It is quite hilly, so expect some tough climbs and fun descents, especially on the extensions. There is a mixture of terrain on this route, but the main route is mainly good stone double track that drains well. You will be exposed up on the ridgetop.

There aren't any big climbs or gnarly descents, but this is still a very nice ride. It is very easy to navigate, and uses some nice tracks, with good views. The trails are pretty good all year round, but it can get muddy in the woods and the chalk is slippery. Puddletown Forest has some nice single track to explore.

Purbeck is a very popular location for mtb'ing, as it offers some superb trails, on some big hills, with some superb views. It does get busy in the summer months, but it is also sticky when wet. The shortcut will allow most riders to attempt this route, and the extension will reward the riders able to do it.

Cyclists have to stay to the main forest tracks, and as these are identical we haven't tried to guide you around a set route. Just pick your spot and ride as much or as little as you like, to wherever you wish to go, using the forest markers (marked on the map) to locate your position. Great for winter/wet rides.

This is a 'classic' Isle of wight ride, with some challenging terrain, and great descents. It is a pretty tough route, but it can be cut in half very easily by using the shortcut. Brighstone Forest is an open access forest, with some great trails in it, including a downhill run at GR 434/851. Hard work in the wet.

mountain bike rides in and around

wiltshire and dorset

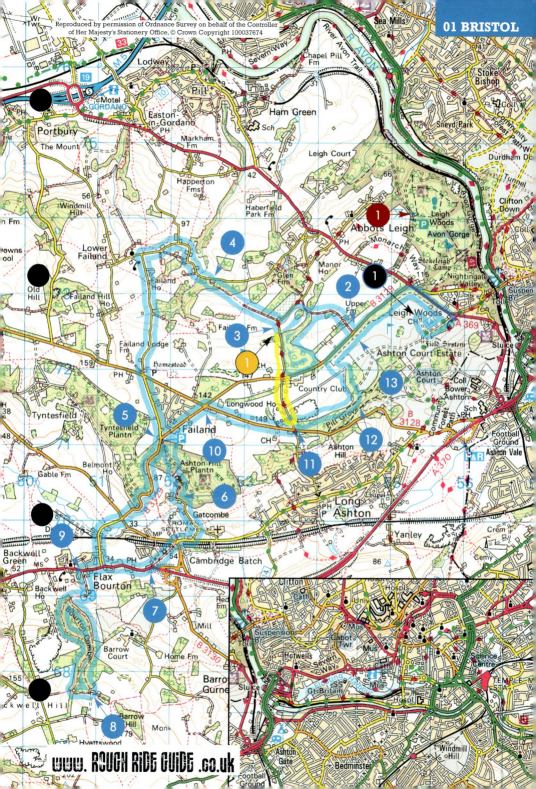

28.2KM (17.5M) 570 metres climbing

1 START. Go back to the arch/entrance to Ashton Court and turn L (signposted) on the Timberland Trail (TT) just before going under the arch (ST 558/727). Follow this rooty, singletrack parallel to the rd, then bearing L (south-west), until a gap in the big wall on your R (545/725).

TOP TIP: Follow the Timberland Trail way markers (a symbol of a tree) when you see them.

2 Go through this and L on the rd (fast) then shortly R on a drive, past Upper farm, and keep SA on the BW. After 0.65km (0.4m) turn L on the TT (539/728), at the start of the woods, and follow this twisty trail through the (50 Acre) woods until you emerge at a rd (535/725).

3 Turn R, DH, on this rd (leaving the TT), or see the shortcut. After 0.15km, where the rd turns R, you keep SA/L on a BW track (535/726), past Orchard Lodge. Follow this BW UH, then becoming a rocky DH, to a rd (525/732) and turn L on this.

4 Follow this rd, UH, bearing L, for 1.3km (0.8m) then turn L on 'Oxhouse Lane' (516/735) for 1.6km (1m) to a X-rds and go SA on 'Flax Bourton Road'. 0.55m to a T-J with a 'B' rd (519/711) and go SA into the car park / entrance to Ashton Hill Plantation.

5 Bear L on the track through a wooden gate, following the perimeter stone wall / LHS. After 0.3km (0.2m) at a X-tracks, go SA, DH, to a main fire road and turn L on this, until the trail levels and you come to a 3-way junction. Turn R then L onto a tarmac rd and L as you leave the woods (521/703).

6 Follow this rd DH for 0.5km (0.3m) then turn R on a rd, over a bridge to a main rd (523/698). Turn R on this, past a car showroom, to a roundabout (521/697) and go SA on Old Weston Rd, to the main rd/A370 (517/ 694) and turn R on this, into Flax Bourton.

7 After 0.9km (0.55m) (or 0.25km if joining from the extension) turn L on a BW/lane (Bourton Combe) (508/693). Follow this R, into the woods, to a BW fork (506 /690) and turn L. Keep L at the next fork, and follow this BW, UH, for 1.45km (0.9m) to a T-J at the top (509/677).

8 Turn R for 0.25km (0.15m) then R on a BW (507/677) before leaving the woods, rocky descent for 0.9m (keep L), to a fork after 1.45km (0.9m) (505/688) and bear R, UH, back to the track you entered the woods on, and follow it back to the main rd (A370) in Flax Bourton (508/693).

9 Turn R on this for 0.25km (0.15m), then L on Station Road (511/694), and follow this for 0.8km (0.5m) back to the X-rds (513/700). Go SA on the B3129 for 2.25km (1.4m), tough climb up Belmont Hill, (past Ashton Hill Plantation), to a X-rds with traffic lights (525/715).

10 Turn R on the B3128 (take care - fast rd), for 1.3km (0.8m), then L at a X-roads (on Longwood Lane). Shortly turn R through a gap to the LHS of a metal gate, (opposite a quarry entrance on L), into Ashton Court (537/713).

11 Immediately turn L on some ST alongside the fence / quarry, (part of the TT again), and follow the marker posts for MTB trail. Join a main fire road after 1km (0.6m), and continue to the L for 0.5km (0.3m) to the south-east corner of a meadow (544/716) and turn L (north) UH on a rocky trail just inside the LHS of the woods (or an easier DT on the LHS, outside the woods).

12 Follow this around the edge of the woods, UH, to a T-J with a wide gravel track at the top (544/720). Turn L (south-west) then very shortly the first R (north-west) on a trail alongside a fence (and horse jumps to the R) and into the woods (542/721). Turn R and follow this rocky, rooty, singletrack alongside a wall on your L, back around the perimeter of Ashton Court.

13 Rejoin the TT by the gap in the wall, but staying in Ashton Court along the track you came along at the start (wall on LHS). Reatrace your tyre tracks, along this trail, bearing R, and emerging by the arch / entrance of Ashton Court (558/727). Turn R along the driveway, then first R, UH, back to the car park (and cafe) (554/727).

SHORTCUT:
-16.7KM (10.4M) -395 metres climbing

1 Turn L on this rd, UH, to a X-rds with the main rd at the top (535/719) and go SA on Longwood Lane, opposite. After 0.65km (0.4m) turn L through a gap at the side of a metal gate (opposite quarry entrance on the R) (537/713) in to Ashton Court and rejoin the main route at no.11.

DIY ROUTE:
Various

The Bristolians (and local wildlife) have created miles and miles of superb single track trails and it is well worth exploring Leigh Woods, Ashton Court, Abbots Pool (by Glen farm), 50 Acre Woods (by the shortcut), and Ashton Hill plantation. The way marked Timberland trail is a good way to start exploring the area, but to discover this areas full potential you need to tag along with a local group ride to find the more elusive trails. There are tracks suitable for families to ride, in Ashton Court and Leigh woods.

TOP TIP: See www.bristolmountainbikeclub.com or ask the local bike shops about group rides.

▪ NOTE: Most of Ashton Court and the Forestry Commission woods are open to cyclists, but the southern part of Leigh Woods is owned by the National Trust and MTB'ers must stay to the main tracks.

GETTING THERE: This ride starts from the Pitch and Putt car park in Ashton Court. Exit the M5 at junction 19 and follow the A369 towards Bristol, then just before the turning (left) to the suspension bridge, turn right through the Arch into Ashton Court. Take the 1st right, up the hill to the car park / Pitch and Putt hut / cafe (554/727). If this is full, go back down the small hill and turn right to the a (rough surfaced) car park on the left here.

ACCOMMODATION: Avon Gorge Hotel, near Clifton suspension bridge, on 0117 973 8955, There is a good YHA right in centre of Bristol on 0117 9221659. There is a wide choice of places to stay in Bristol, and its worth calling the Bristol TI on 0117 9260767 or visiting the website www.visitbristol.co.uk

BIKE SHOPS: Lots in Bristol, Mud Dock (with a cafe) on 0117 929 2151 and Dave Baters on Park St 929 7368 and Bike off Queen's rd in Clifton 293500.

REFRESHMENTS: Cafe at the start / car park, and an ice cream van near at the overflow car park (GR 554/724). On the ride there are pubs at Failand and Flax Bourton. There is lots more choice in Bristol, including Mud Docks (bike shop) cafe upstairs.

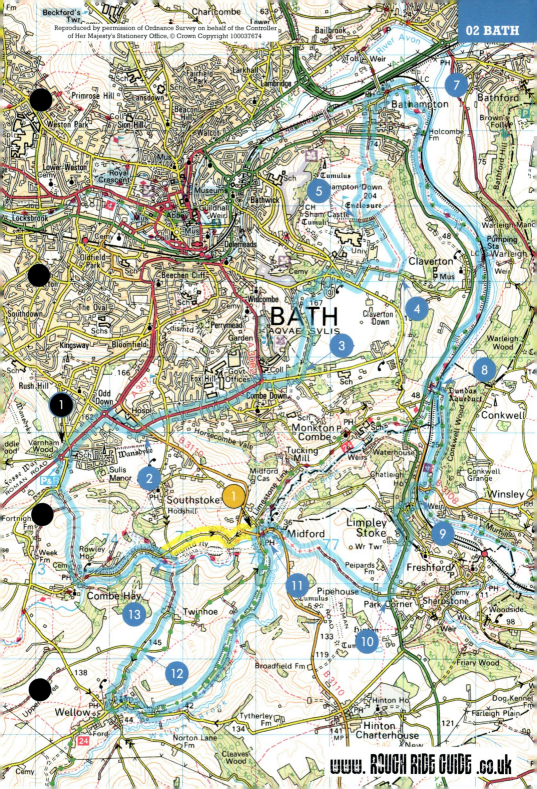

29.5KM (18.3M) 640 metres climbing

❶ START. Go back to the roundabout and turn R on the A367 (into Bath), past the New Burns house pub, **for 0.9km** (0.55m) **to a roundabout** (ST 739/622) and turn R (Frome). Follow Frome rd around to the L and across the B3110 (744/621), to become Bradford Rd (but is also still the A3062).

❷ After 1.8km (1.1m) (Bradford Rd has become North Rd) keep SA on North Rd as the A3062 bears L (north) on Ralph Allen Drive. After 0.5km (0.3m) turn L (opposite Shaft rd) through black metal gates (SP Uni), (766/628) on a gravel track.

❸ Follow this gravel track to a rd (769/641) and turn R (Claverton rd) to a wonky T-J and turn R (effectively SA), then shortly L on Norwood Av, towards the Uni (774/640). **Turn R on the BW** in front of the Uni, alongside the rd, **then turning L** (779/641).

❹ Follow this gravel track alongside the car park (Uni on the L and a field on the R), gradual UH, through the trees **to a golf course at the top** (776/649). Turn L along field edge, on the BW, **to a DT** (774/648) (by a round corrugated building) and turn R, UH, on this.

❺ Follow the BW signs (L then R), across a golf course, over a green and **through a gate, off the golf course.** Bear R on a grassy sunken track to the bottom R (by woods) and a BW sign (775/655).

❻ Follow this on a **steep rocky DH, to a rd and go SA** (Village centre) and follow this to a T-J at the bottom (775/663). Turn R on Bathhampton lane and go over the bridge then turn R on the cycle path 4, alongside the canal (778/665).

❼ Follow this good track alongside the canal **for 4.8km** (3m), then turn R to cross the bridge, following the NCT. Keep following the NCT path as it bears L over the Dundas Aqueduct (785/625).

• **NOTE:** You can follow the Sustrans route no.24 from here, to Midford, to avoid the technical descent on the Pipehouse ByW, if you desire.

❽ Follow this cycletrack for another 1.6km (1m) along the canal, **to bridge no175** (784/613) then bear R, up to the rd, leaving the cyclepath. Turn R on the rd, DH, under a railway bridge and immediately turn L (782/613), to Limpey Stoke.

❾ After 0.25km (0.15m) turn R past a (good) pub (781/611), steep UH, **to the A36** (780/610). Turn L on the path alongside this rd **for 1.3km** (0.8m) **to a X-rds** (778/599) and turn R (Pipehouse).

❿ Keep SA on the ByW which becomes a very technical rocky descent **to the B3110 rd** (763/607). Turn R on this rd into Midford, over the water and turn L to join 'Route 24' Colliers Way, on the disused railway track, or see the *shortcut*.

▪ **NOTE:** The entrance to this trail was closed / changing at the time we were there, but look for the Hope and Anchor pub and you should find it around there.

⓫ Follow this cyclepath for 3.2km (2m) to a rd in Wellow (744/583) and turn R, UH, to a X-rds just past the church (741/584). Turn R on Farm Lane (opposite the Primary school), UH, **for 1km** (0.6m) to some X-rds at the top and go SA.

⓬ 0.65km (0.4m) down to Twinhoe farm and just after the rd bears R, turn L on a BW, through a wooden gate (748/596). Keep SA on this rocky track, DH, over a small bridge and bear L, UH to rd (747/604) and turn L on it.

13 Follow this for 1.3km (0.8m) to the Wheatsheaf pub and turn R (736/600) of the driveway. **13A** Follow this past some stables, on a tough DT climb. Bears L, DH, then UH on a broken concrete rd, to a good rd and turn R on this and follow it back **to the roundabout and the Park and Ride** (733616).

SHORTCUT:

-4.6KM (2.85M) -140 metres climbing

❶ Keep SA at the X-rds immediately after the bridge, for 0.25m (0.15m) to another X-rds (758/607) and turn L and follow this rd for 2.6km (1.6m) to the Wheatsheaf pub in Combe Hay and turn R on the driveway and rejoin the main route at no.13A.

GETTING THERE: This ride starts from the Park and Ride off the A367, on the southern edge of Bath (733/616). The car park is closed on Sunday, but you can easily park on the roads here, or park at the University. There is a train station in Bath.

ACCOMMODATION: There is lots of choice of accomodation in Bath. Speak to the Bath Tourist Info office on 0906 7112000 (50p a minute) for more information. Also, YHA in Bath (near the university) on 0870 770 5688, Camping at Newton Mill Camping & Caravan on 01225 333909 or Bath Marina & Caravan Park on 01225 424301 (both in Bath).

BIKE SHOPS: John's Bikes on Walcot St (GR 751/652) in Bath on 01225 334633 is good.

REFRESHMENTS: There is lots of choice in and around Bath, as well as pubs in Limpley Stoke, Midford, Wellow, Combe Hay on the route.

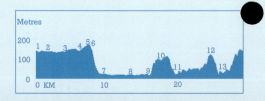

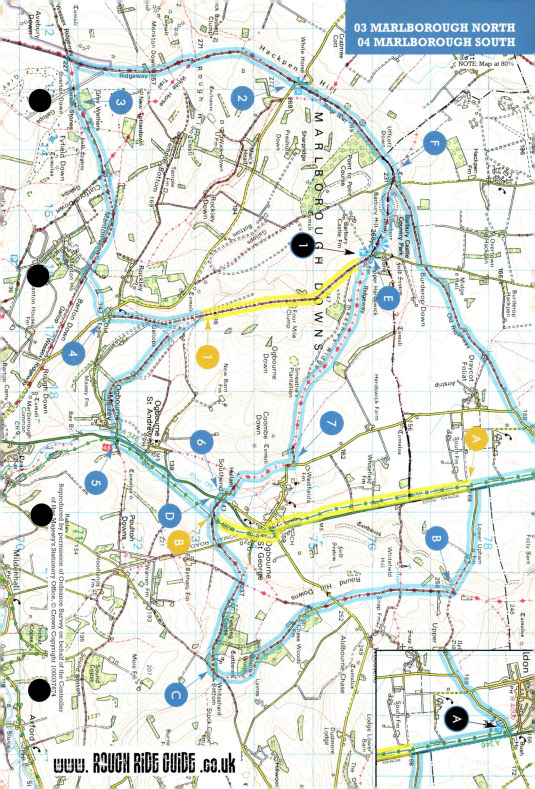

NORTH ROUTE

25KM (15.5) 400 metres of climbing

1 START. Go west, to/through Barbury Castle, on a BW, DH to a rd and turn R, then immediately L on the Ridgeway (SU 145/764). 2.4km (1.5m) to a rd (129/747), and go SA into car park (White Horse on the hillside here).

2 Go along the Ridgeway for 4.2km (2.6m) at a X-tracks and a board welcoming you to Fyfield Down Nature Reserve (125/709) turn L over a gate into the Nature Reserve. Head over grassy BW for 0.5km (0.3m) then across the Gallops on to a gravel track.

3 UH on this track to a gate, and keep SA, DH to the valley bottom and go R. After 1.1km (0.7m) go L on a BW (161/ 711), 0.15km past a DT BW on the L, DH to a rd (168/714) and go L on it, then bear R on a track.

4 Immediately crossing a rd, keep SA on a good track for 1.45km (0.9m) to a X-tracks (168/730). Turn R, UH, on a ByW or see shortcut. Past the gallops, DH, to corner of a rd in Ogbourne Maizey and keep SA/L to A346 (188/716)

5 Cross this rd to the cycletrack on the other side, by a metal bridge, and turn L on this cycletrack (old railway). Follow this for 2.1km (1.3m) to where the Ridgeway crosses you (201/733) and go L on this, DH to the A346 rd.

6 Go SA on the rd opposite, UH, past the houses to a T-J (194/738), and turn R (north) and follow this to a rd. Go SA/L on the rd, then shortly turn L (west) off it, back off-road on the Ridgeway (192/747).

7 Follow the Ridgeway, UH, for 4km (2.5m) to a T-J (158 /759) at the top and turn R. Just up here turn L through a single gate (opposite the farm, and before the Frog & Spoon cafe) on a BW, back to the car park (157/761).

SHORTCUT:
-7.25KM (4.5M) -140 metres climbing

1 Keep SA on this good track, UH, for another 3.2km (2m) (becoming tarmac at the end, and Ridgeway joins from the R), past the Frog and Spoon cafe on the R and turn L through a gate back to the car park (157/761).

SOUTH ROUTE

24.1KM (15M) 380 metres of climbing

A START. Go south on 'Chiseldon to Marlborough' cycle path, for 1.6km (1m), then go L to the A346 rd (SU 196/777) or see the shortcut. Turn L on this rd, then shortly R to Lower Upham farm. Go past the farm, on a stoney track, UH, to a X-tracks with Ridgeway at top (213/774).

B Turn R (south) on the Ridgeway, for 2km (1.25m) to a rd (215/ 754) and go SA on the drive. Continue on this past the farm (or stay on the Ridgeway to -2.4km/1.5m), DH, bearing R, to a DT at the bottom, turn R, then shortly R again at a fork (227/733)

C Follow this UH, to the top and keep SA, then just before you start descending bear L following the Ridgeway signposts, DH. To a minor rd and keep SA, and follow this down to the main rd (198/734) or see shortcut.

D Go SA on the Ridgeway, UH, to a T-J (194/738) and turn R (north) and follow this to a rd and go SA/L on the rd. Shortly turn L (west) back off-road, on the Ridgeway and follow this DT, UH for about 4km (2.5m) to a T-J (158/759) at the top and turn R.

E Shortly turn L through a single gate (opposite the farm, and before the cafe) on a BW, past a car park (157/761). Through a gate on a grassy track through Barbury Castle, DH to a rd. Turn R, then R again on a ByW (Old Ridgeway Chiseldon).

F DH, 1.45km (0.9m) to a rd and tun L then R (effectively SA) back onto the ByW (159/769). Follow this rough track, and keep SA as it becomes tarmac, joining a rd and keep SA/L. 0.4km (0.25m) to a X-rds and go SA then just past New Farm go R, back to the car park (193/793).

SHORTCUT:
2 options

Use the cyclepath between Ogbourne St George and Chiseldon on either the outward or return leg of the route:

A -5.2km/3.2m & 160 metres of climbing

B -6.6km/4.1m & 155 metres of climbing

GETTING THERE: Train station in Swindon, follow the Sustrans cycle route no.45 from the station, for 13km/8m to Chiseldon.

East route starts from a car park by Chiseldon - exit the M4 at junction 15, go south on the A346 for 1 mile, then turn R at a X-roads (just past the petrol station), and the car park (height restriction) is on the left (192/793).

West route starts at Barbury Castle - follow the B4005 through Chiseldon and turn L on a RHB, to Barbur Castle car park (157/761).

BIKE SHOPS: There is plenty of choice in Swindon e.g. Mitchell Cycles on 01793 523306, Swindon Cycles on 01793 700105 and Red Planet Bikes on 01793 522211.

ACCOMMODATION: B&B at Manor Farm in Avebury on 01672 539294 B&B at Browns Farm in Marlborough on 01672 515129 Crockford@Farming.co.uk Marlborough TI on 01672 513989 Wiltshire Cycling hotline (with accomodation info) on 01980 623255

REFRESHMENTS: East route: Pub in Chiseldon and a cafe at the Esso garage, and a cafe by Barbury Castle. West route: cafe at Barbury castle and a pub in Ogbourne St Andrew.

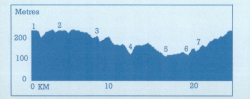

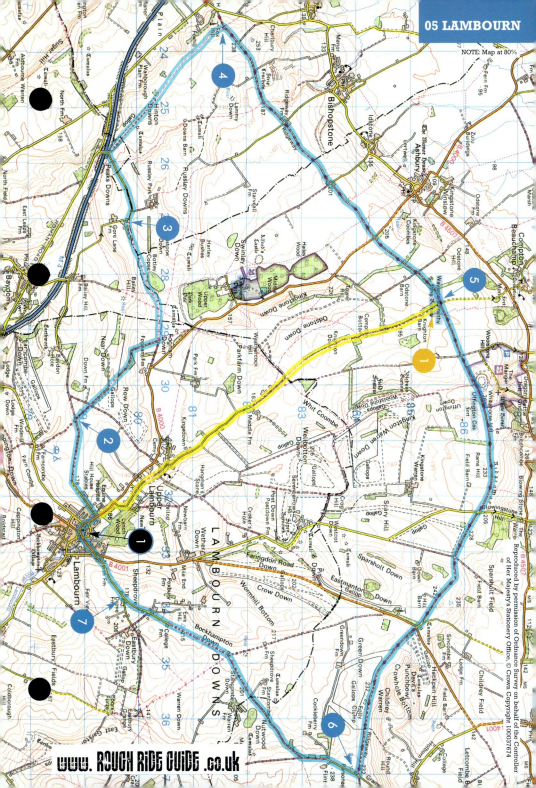

34.6KM (21.5M) 490 metres of climbing

1 START. From the X-rds in the centre of the village (SU 326/789) by the church, head north on Parsonage lane, for 0.5km (0.3m), then turn L on Folly rd (323/792). Keep SA on this for 1.95km (1.2m) becoming a ByW, to a X-tracks (306/788) and turn R.

2 Keep SA after 0.3km (0.2m) at another X-tracks, for 0.5km (0.3m) and keep SA on a feint ByW track, as the DT bears L (300/794). 1.4km (0.85m) to a X-tracks (292/803) and turn L on the ByW, and keep SA for 2.35KM (1.45m) to a rd, by a bungalow (270/798).

3 Keep SA on the Ridgeway for 16km/10m to a minor rd (370/840) and rejoin the main route at no.6 or read on for more detailed information. Go SA/R on the rd for 1.4km (0.85m), then turn R on the BW (258/794) just before the bridge over the M4. Turn R immediately through a single gate, then turn L on a feint track (alongside the Gallop - an area for horses). Keep SA for 3.1km (1.95m), towards the satellite tower, and turn R behind the barn on the Ridgeway (235/815).

4 2.1km (1.3m) to a rd and go SA, (water tap on the L, after 1.4km (0.85m) by the barns), for another 2.75km (1.7m) to the B4000 rd (273/843. Go SA for 0.6m to a X-tracks and go SA for 0.7km (0.45m) past the neolithic Weyland Smithy burial mound, from around 2800BC at (280/853) to a X-tracks (285/ 855) and keep SA for 4km (2.5m) to a rd or see the shortcut.

5 Go SA at the rd (322/862), for 1km (0.6m) to a X-tracks and go SA, UH (track splits, but rejoins shortly) for 1.65km (1m) to a rd. Bear R on this minor rd, to the B4001 rd (343/851) and go SA on the Ridgeway, for another 3km (1.9m) to a minor rd (370/840).

6 Turn R on this rd, for 0.65km (0.4m) to a fork just past a farm, and bear L on the ByW, for 0.5km (0.3m) to a X-tracks (367/829) and turn R. 1.45km (0.9m), and keep SA on the concrete track, UH, for 0.8km (0.5m) to a barn (348/816). Keep SA on the concrete track for 2.25km (1.4m) where a rd joins from the L (338/797).

7 Turn R into the field on the RHS of the rd, behind the hedge, bearing L, DH, parallel to the rd. This rejoins the rd, and keep you SA, DH, to the B4001 rd and bear L on this for 0.5km (0.3m) back to the X-rds in the centre of Lambourn (326/789), and go SA, back to the car park.

SHORTCUT:
-9.2KM (5.7M) -240 metres of climbing

1 Turn R at the X-tracks, DH, for 3.2km (2m) to a X-tracks, and go SA on a DT. After 2.75km (1.7m) past Maddle farm, bear R with the rd to a T-J (314/805).

2 Turn L, for 0.1km (0.05m) bear R to the B4000 rd (313/803) and turn L on this for 1.95km (1.2m) to a X-rds in Lambourn (326/789), and turn R back to the car park.

The Ridgeway makes up the backbone of this ride.

GETTING THERE: Start from the village of Lambourn, which is just north of junction 14 of the M4, on the B4000 (and B4001). There is a car park near the library, and some spaces outside the church. Nearest train station is in Swindon - follow Sustrans cyclepath no45 for 12km/8m over M4, past Badbury then left past Lidington castle and keep SA to Fox hill/no.4.

ACCOMMODATION: B&B in Shefford Woodlands (by junction 14 of the M4) on 01488 648466, and B&B's in Letcombe Regis on: 01235 762860 and 01235 765827. Camping (nr Lambourn) at Farncombe farm on: 01488 71833. Wantage T.I. on: 01235 760176 or Newbury T.I. on: 01635 30267

BIKE SHOP: Ridgeway Cycles in Wantage on tel: 01235 764 445

REFRESHMENTS: There is a pub and a shop in Lambourn, a water tap at GR 264/835. There are no pubs or shops on the route, but there are some just off the (northern side of the) Ridgeway.

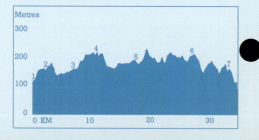

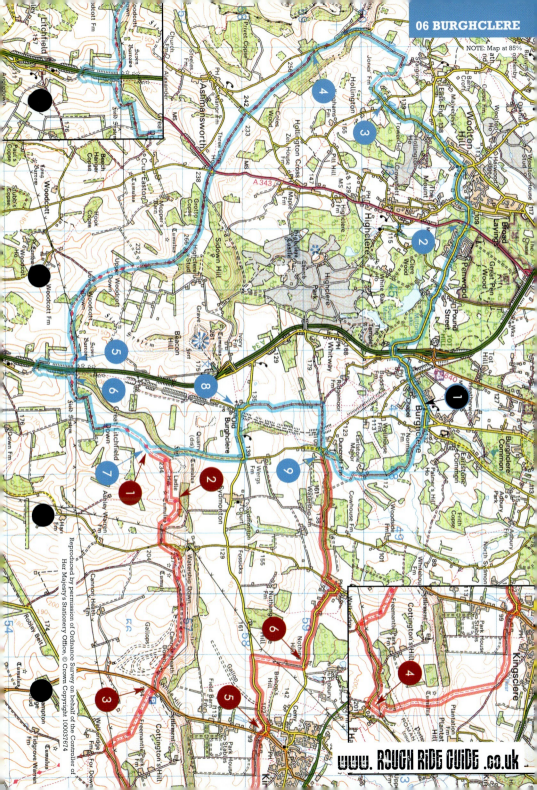

27.4 (17M) 490 metres of climbing

① START. Go back to the main (Harts) rd and go L on it for 1.1km (0.7m), through Burghclere, bearing L, and take 2nd R (bridge over the A34 rd). Follow this rd for 2.7km (1.7m) to a X-rds (with A343) and go SA (Highclere).

② 0.25km (0.15m) to a T-J (SU 436/618) and turn L on this rd for 0.8km (0.5m), then turn L on Church Rd (by the church) (430/617). 0.7km (0.45m) to a fork in the rd, and bear L (Hollington), 1km (0.65m) to a grass triangle and bear R, then SA/L on a BW (rd) (419/603).

③ Becomes off-road, and bears R to the corner of a track (413/606) and turn L on this. Keep L, UH to a rd (407/599) and turn L on this for 0.8km (0.5m), then bear L on the Wayfarers Walk (WW), ByW (410/592).

Quick guide: Stay on 'Wayfarers walk' for 7.6km (4.7m) to the A34 rd (463/551) and rejoin the route at no.5.

④ 2.8km (1.75m) to the A343 rd (430/575), bear L then R back on the WW. After 2.25km (1.4m) (going DH), bear R after the metal gates as the DT bears L, to the top of the field. Through a field to some metal gates and bear L, into the woods, to the A34 rd (462/551).

⑤ Turn R just before the rd, which bears L under the bridge (A34) and immediately turn L into a field (not signposted) (462/545). Follow the LHS of the field (parallel to the rd) for 0.8km (0.5m) (old bridge on the L), then turn R, up the valley (463/551).

⑥ After 1.2km (0.75m), turn L on another DT, following the white wooden arrow (472/555), near some woods. After 1.1km (0.7m) on this, bear L at a very feint fork (476/564), before the top of the hill, or see the *extension*.

⑦ DH, to the LHS of the hill top, going north, along the BW track for 1.6km (1m) to a rd (477/579). Turn L, into Old Burghclere, over a bridge, bearing R, then keep SA on the ByW, as the rd bears L, (468/580).

⑧ 1.2km (0.75m) to a X-tracks (469/593) and turn R, for 0.8km (0.5m), to a rd and turn L, then immediately bear R at the rd fork, then turn immediately L on a BW (477/593), before another rd T-J.

⑨ 0.7km (0.45m) to a DT and turn L on this, then shortly R on the BW (if this is overgrown - follow the DT, past the manor, and rejoin the BW. Follow this to a X-rds at a grass triangle, (472/610) and go SA (Church lane) back to the car (470/610).

EXTENSION:

+17.2KM (10.7M) +320 metres climbing

① Bear R at the fork (staying on the WW), then shortly, keep SA through the gates, as track bears R. To the top of the hill and bear R on grassy a DT, to a T-J and turn (sharp) L for 0.15km then turn R through the wooden gate, by a green gate (484/568).

② Through the field, and bear L at a metal gate, onto a good track (under the elec. cables), UH to a rd (491/566). Go SA on a ST BW, UH through some wooden gates, and join a DT, bearing L and follow this for 1.95km (1.2m), to a rd (515/564).

③ Turn L on the rd, then immediately (sharp) R on the (WW) BW and follow this for 1.3km (0.8m) to a rd (525/556). Turn L on the rd (leaving the WW) for 0.9m, then turn L on a BW through some metal gates (538/558), just before entering Hannington village.

④ Bear sharp L at end of the field, and keep SA/L for 2km (1.25m) to a T-J (535/580) at the end of a path through the middle of a field Turn L, to a fork and bear L on the ST, and keep SA, becoming a drive, to a rd.

⑤ Turn R on the rd, then immediately L on Bear Hill rd (by some houses), over the stream, to a T-J (522/583). Turn L on this rd (Sydmonton) for 1.2km (0.75m), then turn R on a BW (large stone in the middle) (510/581), for 0.8km (0.5m) to a rd (512/589).

⑥ Turn L on the rd for 1.5km (0.95m) to a T-J in Ecchinswell village, (Royal Oak pub here), and turn L, for 0.25km (0.15m) then turn R on another rd (497/593) (Burchclere). After 2.25km (1.4m) bear R at the fork (477/593), and immediately turn R again on a BW (before the blue HGV sign) and rejoin the main route at no.9.

GETTING THERE: Start in Burghclere, just off the A34, south of Newbury. Follow the signs for Burghclere off the A34 and go through the village, past the Carpenters Arms pub, then turn R on Church lane (by the church) and park in the lay-by on the left just here (470/610). Train station in Newbury - go south on A339 then SA/south at a roundabout, to Burghclere.

ACCOMMODATION: B&B in Burchclere on: 01635 278305, B&B in Newtown on: 01635 43097, Camping at Oakley farm (off the A343), on: 01635 36581. Newbury T.I. on: 01635 30167

BIKE SHOP: Cycle Shop in Newbury on: 01635 582100

REFRESHMENTS: Pub in Burghclere, just off the route in Woolton hill and Ashmansworth. More in Hannington, Kingsclere & Ecchinswell on the extension.

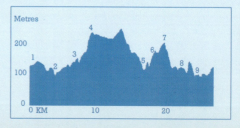

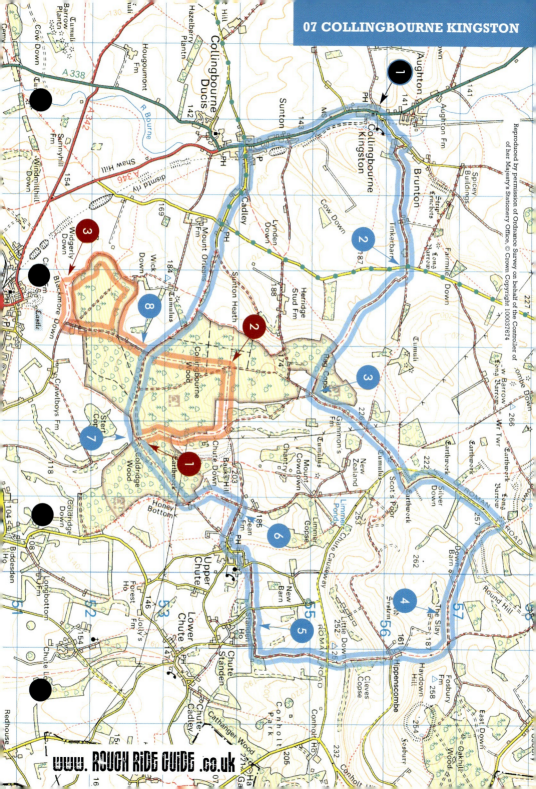

22.8KM (14.2M) 450 metres of climbing

1 START. Turn L (south) on the A338 rd towards Collingbourne Kingston and turn L on the rd (SU 239/559) to Brunton. After 0.55km (0.35m) along this rd turn R (243/563) on a BW, UH, for 1.8km (1.1m) to a rd (259/563).

2 Go SA on track opposite, then shortly at a fork (261/563) bear R and follow this DH, to a gate at the bottom of the valley (270/553) and go through this, UH, (woods on the R) on a feint track. Into the wood and up to a main track (276/550).

3 Turn L on this for 1.6km (1m) to a rd and go L (north) on this for another 1.6km (1m) then turn R on a BW (294/576). Follow this BW, UH, then DH, for 1.85km (1.15m) to a X-tracks (309/569) of BW's and turn R (south), for a steep DH.

4 DH, through the farm, past a house, to a minor rd (311/561) and turn L on this, then immediately R (south). Tough UH for 0.9km (0.55m) to a rd and go SA on the BW, DH, turning R (west) after 1km (0.6m), and keep SA (west) as the track shortly turns L (south), to a rd.

5 Keep SA on the BW, to another rd (299/542) and turn L on this, then immediately R on another rd (west). DH, to a grass triangle (297/539) and turn R (west), keeping SA, past the pub, on to a ByW.

6 0.4km (0.25m), DH, to a X-tracks (291/540) and turn left (south) on the RUPP, following the edge of the woods to Honey Bottom (291/533). Turn R past the barrier, into the woods for 0.7m to a X-tracks (282/526) and go SA on the ST BW or see the extension.

7 Follow this BW as it bears R, along the edge of the wood, rejoining the wide forest track by a barrier. Continue along this forest track, (ignoring a R turn), to a X-tracks (271/528) where the track turns L, and keep SA, along the edge of the woods.

8 Exit the wood after 0.8km (0.5m), DH, to a rd and keep SA on this, to a X-rds (254/538) and pub. Go SA for 1.1km (0.7m) to a X-rds in Collingbourne Ducis (244/541). Turn R on the A338 rd, through Collingbourne Kingston, and back to your car (236/568).

EXTENSION:

+6.5KM (4M) +100 metres of climbing

1 Turn R (north) and follow this BW along the edge of the woods for 1.3km (0.8m) and turn L on a (BW) track opposite a gate on the R. Follow this ST for 0.8km (0.5m) to a X-tracks (273/539) and turn L then immediately R on ST BW into woods.

2 Exit woods after 1.1km (0.7m) and keep SA for another 0.5km (0.3m) (to start of woods again) and turn R (269/524) on a DT, to a gate. Go to the L of the gate and follow the nice ST which stays close to the RHS of the woods, for 2.1km (1.3m), and out onto grassy track.

3 Turn L (SA) and follow this to a grassy DT BW (262/517) and turn L (east) for 0.5km (0.3m) to a better track (267/516) and turn L (north) into the woods, for 1.2km (0.75m) to a X-rds (271/528) (been here before) and turn L (along egde of woods), rejoin the main route at no.8.

•**NOTE**: There are some other nice tracks to explore in Collingbourne Woods.

GETTING THERE: This ride starts from Collingbourne Kingston, off the A338 (236/568). Exit the M4 at junction 15 and head south on the A346, which changes to the A338 at the roundabout in Burbage, south to Collingbourne Kingston. There is a lay-by half a mile north of the village which is suitable to pak in. There is a train station in Pewsey, about 3 miles west of the west route.

ACCOMMODATION: Manor Farm B&B in Collingbourne Kingston on 01264 850859, York Lodge B&B in Andover on 01264 781313. YHA in Salisbury on 0870 770 6018. Andover TI on 01264 324320

BIKE SHOPS: Bolton's Bikes on 01264 791818, Just Bikes on 355982 and Behind the Bike Shed on 338794, all in Andover. Also, Bikes and Boards in Devizes on 01380 729621.

REFRESHMENTS: Pubs at Upper Chute, Cadley (plus a shop), and Collingbourne Ducis.

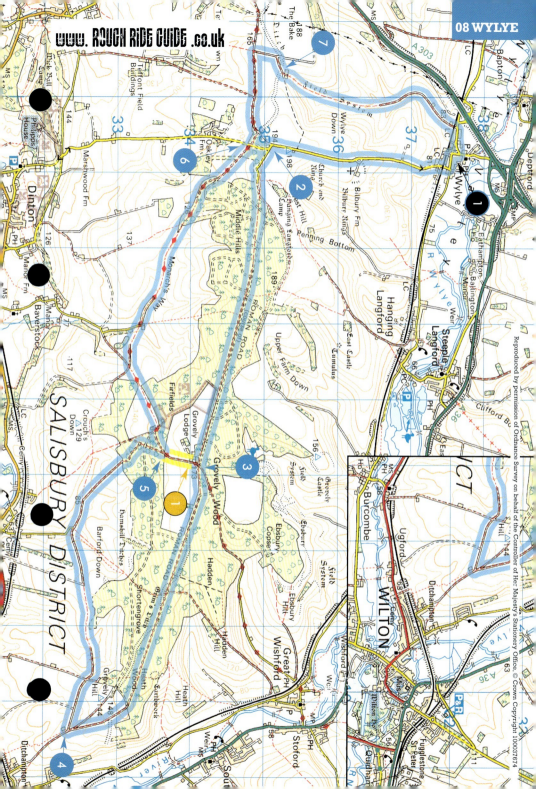

26KM (16.1M) 425 metres of climbing

A START. By the church in Wylye (SU 008/377), go south on the High St to a X-rds and turn L (east) on Fore St. After 0.25km (0.15m) turn R on Dinton rd (010/375), UH, on this rd for 2.6km (1.6m) to a fork (007/351) just past a LHB by the woods and bear L (east) on the rd.

B After 0.65km (0.4m) when it has become a gravel track bear R onto a BW (013/349). Go across 3 fire roads, until you join a fire road head-ong east (022/349). Follow this track for 2.75km (1.7m) to a X-tracks at Grovely Lodge (049/341) and keep SA or see the shortcut.

C 0.4km (0.25m) come to a DT and go SA/R on this, keep SA at a X-tracks after 1.4km (0.85m). Exit the woods, and go DH, for 0.9km (0.55m) to a track (off-set X-tracks) (084/324) and go L then R (i.e. 2nd R) before the building.

D Follow this for 2.8km (1.75m) as it traverses the hillside to the end of a rd (057/324) and keep R on the main track. 0.4km (0.25m) to a fork (053/325) and bear R, UH into a wood, to a T-J and go R, SA at a X-tracks to a T-J (047/336) and go L.

E After 0.3km (0.2m) bear R with the track in front of a house (044/335), to a fork and bear L, DH for 0.9km (0.55m) to a X-tracks (036/332). Turn R 0.55km (0.35m) to a barn and tarmac rd, and keep SA on the Monarchs way and follow this for 2.9km (1.8m) to a rd (006/348).

F Go SA for another 1.3km (0.8m) on the Monarchs way to a X-tracks (ST 994/349) and turn R on the gravel track. After 0.3km (0.2m) at a fork in front of a big green storage tank (995/352), bear R on this track for 0.25km (0.15m) to another fork with a barn to the L (997353) and bear L, DH, (barn to your L), down through valley.

G After 2.8km (1.75m) (joined a surfaced track and crossed the railway) at a rd back in Wylye (SU 004/376), turn R. To a fork and keep L on Dyer Lane (Teapot St R) back to the High St (008/377) by the church and the Bell pub.

SHORTCUT:

-8.4KM (5.2M) -140 metres of climbing

A Turn R through 'No through road' signs for 0.5km (0.3m) to fork and bear R and rejoin the main route at no.5.

Dappled doubletrack north of Oakley farm

GETTING THERE: This route starts in the small village of Wylye, north-west of Salisbury, where the A303 and A36 roads cross. Follow the sign-posts to Wylye, where there is parking for a few cars in the village. Train station in Salisbury - follow the cyclepath (5km/3m) to Wilton and join the ride from there (see map).

ACCOMMODATION: B&B at The Bell Inn in Wylye, on 01985 248338, B&B in Sherrington on 01985 850453, YHA in Salisbury on 0870 770 6018 Camping: Hudsons Field (nr Old Sarum) in Salisbury, 01722 320 713 Wiltshire cyclist friendly accomodation info on 01980 623255 and , Salisbury TI on 01722 334956 Warminster TI on 01985 218548

BIKE SHOPS: Stonehendge Cycleworks 01722 334915, Mitchells Cycles on 01793 616012, Hills Cycles on 01980 622705 all in Salisbury. Bachelors in Warminster on 01985 213221.

REFRESHMENTS: There is a pub in Wylye for after the ride, but nothing on the ride.

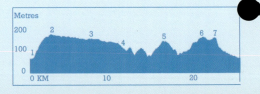

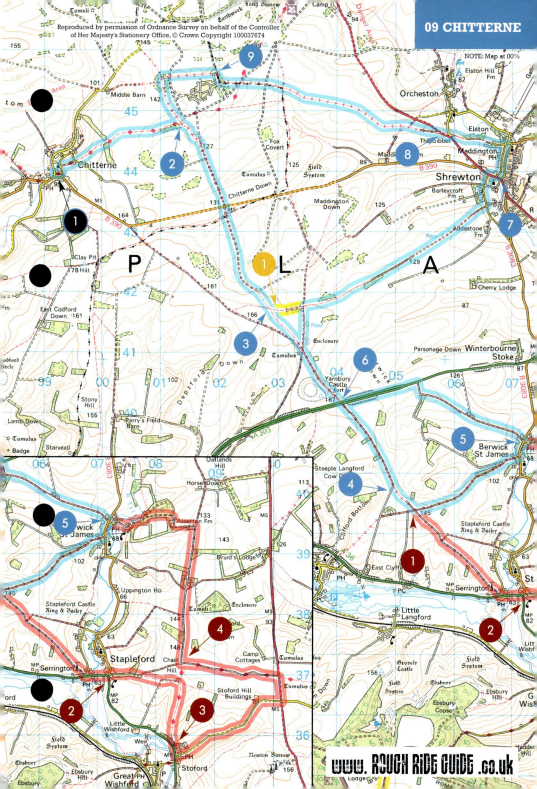

32.5KM (20.2M) 400 metres climbing

❶ START. Go towards the B390 but turn L before it, on a minor rd (ST 992/440) with Imber Range Perimeter Path (IRPP) signpost. Bears L, then shortly turn R on the IRPP, ST, UH (993/441), and keep SA at a minor rd by a barn, for 1.95km (1.2m) to where a ByW crosses you (SU 013/448)

■ **NOTE:** You can now see the 'German Village'. Once Imber village, but during the cold war is was evacuated to make a mock german village, and more recently a Bosnian village. It's still used (and guarded) so just look.

❷ Turn R (south) on the DT (ByW), for 1.6km (1m) to the B390 rd and go SA for another 1m and bear R (SA) on a BW, as the DT bears L. UH, for 0.4km (0.25m) to a (BW) X-tracks (028/417) and keep SA, DH, or see the *shortcut*.

❸ Grassy DT for 0.9km (0.55m) to a X-tracks and keep SA (east of the old fort/mound) for 1.1km (0.7m) to the A303 rd (041/402). Cross this rd carefully and keep SA on a good track (becoming tarmac, past barn) and keep SA / L (on the ByW) as drive bears R.

❹ 0.5km (0.3m) to a X-rds (053/384) (radar tower on R) and turn L on a grassy DT (mast of R) or see the *extension*. DH, for 2.1km (1.3m) emerging by a farm on the L, and keep SA/R on a concrete track to a rd (071/3925) (bus stop SA) in Berwick St James and turn L on this rd for 0.3km (0.2m) then turn L on a BW (072/395).

❺ Keep L at the fork after 1km (0.65m), for another 1km (0.6m) to a T-J and turn R to the main rd (054/405). Turn L on this, for 1.3km (0.8m) then turn R (north) over it, back onto a ByW you came from earlier (041/402).

❻ 1.1km (0.7m) back to the X-tracks and turn R, for 0.7km (0.45m) to another X-tracks (034/418) and turn R. **6A** Follow this BW, DH, for 3.6km (2.25m) to a rd (X-rds) (066/434). Turn L on this rd (The common) to the A360 rd and turn R, then shortly L on Tanners lane (067/439).

❼ 0.55km (0.35m) to a T-J (069/444) and turn L on (The Hollow) rd and keep SA on this as it becomes a BW past the houses. To a rd at the end and turn L to the main rd (059/446), and turn R on this for just 0.25km (0.15m)

then turn L on a ByW (stick to the ROW's along here).

❽ Keep SA (west) for about 4km (2.5m), (ignore all the tracks crossing you), until you come to the 'German village' (020/455). Turn R (north), then L on the ByW, on the northern side of the village (west).

❾ 1km (0.6m), just over a good track to some X-tracks in the trees (010/455), turn L (south), for 0.9km (0.55m) to a X-tracks you were at earlier (013/448). Turn R and retrace your earlier steps, DH, back into Chitterne (ST 992/439).

SHORTCUT:

-11.3KM (7M) -140 metres of climbing

❶ Turn L (east) on the BW, for 0.55km (0.35m), between some trees to a X-tracks (SU 034/418) and go SA, and rejoin the main route at no.6A.

EXTENSION:

+11KM (6.8M) +175 metres climbing

❶ Keep SA, down the other side of the hill, keeping R (south east) to the A36 rd (SU 068/370). Turn L on this rd for 0.4km (0.25m) then as it turns R, turn L on the B3083 then R (effectively SA) on Chain Hill.

❷ After 0.55km (0.35m) keep R at the fork, then joining a track at the outside bend, go SA/L on this 0.3km (0.2m) to a X-tracks (084/369) by a building. Turn R, DH, on the Monarch's Way, to the A36 and go L on this, to Stoford.

❸ Shortly go L on a rd, UH into the valley (pub) for 2.2km (1.35m) to the A360 rd (101/366). Turn L on this rd for 0.4km (0.25m) then L on Monarch's Way BW (101/370), for 1.65km (1m) to a X-tracks (084/372) and go R (north).

❹ Keep SA (north) on this track for 2.4km (1.5m), then turn L (west) to Asserton farm. Bear bear R at the farm, then L on a BW, dropping steeply to cross the river and into Berwick St James (072/395). Go SA on another BW track, and rejoin the main route at no.5.

GETTING THERE: This ride starts from the small village of Chitterne, which lies north west of Salisbury on the B390 rd, between the A360 and A36. There is parking available at the village hall (992/439), opposite the green, near the public telephone. Closest train station is in Warminster (12km/7.5m).

ACCOMODATION: B&B's in Chitterne on 01985 859 269, and Salisbury on 01722 416517. YHA in Salisbury on 0870 770 6018. Camping: Hudsons Field (nr Old Sarum) in Salisbury on 01722 320 713. Salisbury TI on 01722 334956, and Warminster TI on 01985 218548. Also, Wiltshire cyclist friendly accomodation information on 01980 623255.

BIKE SHOPS: Stonehendge Cycleworks on 01722 616012, Mitchells Cycles on 01793 616012, Hills Cycles on 01980 622705 all in Salisbury. Bachelors in Warminster on 01985 213221.

REFRESHMENTS: There are pubs in Chitterne at the start/end, Berwick St James, and Shrewton. There are also pubs on the extension in Stapleford, and Stoford.

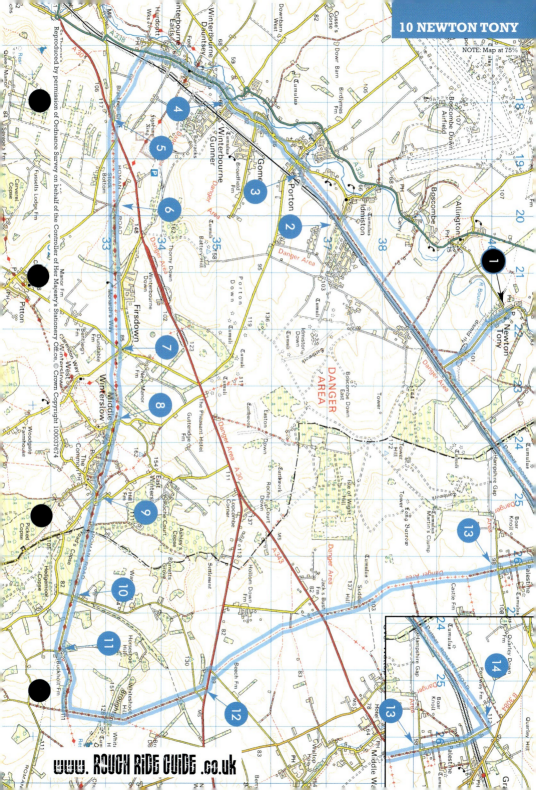

37.2KM (23.1M) 560 metres of climbing

① START. Head SE along the minor road, through the village, to a T-J by the train track (SU 226/391). Turn R on this ByW, and keep SA alongside the railway, for 3.2km (2m) to a tarmac rd (Idmiston) with a large railway bridge to the L (201/372). Turn R on the rd then very shortly turn L on 'Ladyway' as the BW starts on a broken tarmac track.

② Past the static caravans, on a grassy BW, around the L of the field, to a silver metal gate (farm buildings SA). Go through the gate into a field and head to the right of buildings then through a wooden gate to a narrow tarmac track (193/366) and turn R on this track.

③ After 0.15km (0.1m) at a rd, and turn L on this, DH, for 0.15km (0.1m) to a X-rds (190/364) (Porton Hotel pub to the L). Go SA on Gomeldon road, and follow this for 1.8km (1.1m) to a T-J with A338 rd (180/352).

④ Turn L (south) on the A338 rd (SP Salisbury) for 1.95km (1.2m), then turn L on a white gravel BW (opposite sign to the pub on Hurdcott Lane) (171/337). Under a railway bridge, for 1.45km (0.9m) to the A30 rd (184/331) and cross this and go through a small wooden gate.

⑤ Follow this (Roman Road) ByW alongside a line of trees, (east), across the field to some metal gates and a rd. Go SA through another gate, UH, along the right-hand side of a field for 1km (0.6m) to a small wooden gate to a X-tracks (198/332) (very overgrown to the R) and go SA.

⑥ Go over a wide track, into the trees for a 1.3km (0.8m) section of fast DH woodland ST. Emerge from the woods and follow the trail SA, with houses L and fields R, for 1.45km (0.9m) to a rd near a small windmill (223/332).

⑦ Head L on the rd to a X-rds, then R (West Wintersow) for 0.15km (0.1m) then L on a hedge-lined ByW (opposite a silver metal gate). UH, for 0.8m into the woods, then onto a gravel track emerging at the end of Cobb Lane by Middleton Farmhouse (236/332).

⑧ Continue SA down 'Roman Road', bearing slightly to the L past 'Tudor Cottage', and after 0.3km (0.2m) as the main rd bears R, go SA down 'The Causeway'. DH, then bears R slightly around a playground, then turn L past 'Shripple Cottage' and up to a T-junction with 'Red Lane' (248/329).

⑨ Turn R down 'Red Lane' towards the rd, continue down 'Gunville Hill', take a L (SP Stockbridge), then R following a ByW sign down Easton Common Hill (251/328). Follow the gravel trail for 1.8km (1.1m) to a X-rds (267/324).

⑩ Keep SA, UH, on a tarmac track, for 1km (0.6m) to Buckholt Farm (large red-brick house) (277/322). The trail continues SA to the R of the barn (signs to Clarendon) and follow the trail as it bears L to the start of a tree-lined DT (278/323).

⑪ Follow this trail for 1.1km (0.7m) to a X-tracks (287/323) and turn L and follow this trail, bearing L after 1km (0.65m), for 1.45km (0.9m) to a rd. Go SA for 0.15km (0.1m) to T-J with the A30 (283/348) and go L onto this.

⑫ After 0.3km (0.2m) turn turn on another rd, then very shortly L on a BW (281/350). Keep SA on this trail for 2.25km (1.4m), going SA the all the X-tracks, to a rd (270/369). Go SA on the ByW opposite, keeping SA for 3.4km (2.1m) to tarmac X-rds (262/401).

⑬ Go SA on Mt. Hermon Road, through Palestine, for 0.8km (0.5m) to the end of Mt. Hermon Road, where the rd bends R and go SA over a railway bridge. After 0.5km (0.3m) where the rd bends R (258/414), turn L through a long green triangular metal gate, on a BW.

⑭ Follow this BW, which joins alongside a railway line, for 4km (2.5m) back to where you joined this track (226/391), and turn R on the road, for 1.6km (1m), back in to Newton Tony and the car (217/402).

GETTING THERE: This ride starts from Newton Tony, which is just off the A338, north east of Salisbury. Parking is easy here and there is a pub for after the ride, although you could easily start from any of the other villages on the route if its easier. There is a train station in Grateley at the northern point of the route.

ACCOMMODATION: B&B in Salisbury on 01722 328 364 and on 335 419. YHA in Salisbury on 0870 770 6019. Camping at Hudsons Field in Salisbury (nr Old Sarum), 01722 320 713. Salisbury TI on 01722 334956.

BIKE SHOPS: Stonehendge Cycleworks on 01722 334915, Nash's Cycles on 01722 335887 and Hayball & Co on 01722 411378 - all in Salisbury.

REFRESHMENTS: There is a pub at the start/end in Newton Tony, The Porton Hotel pub in Porton, and a pub and post office/convenience store in Winterbourne Dauntsey, all early on, then a pub in Middle Winterslow about half-way, and a pub in Grateley towards the end.

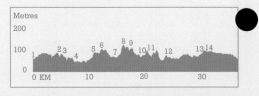

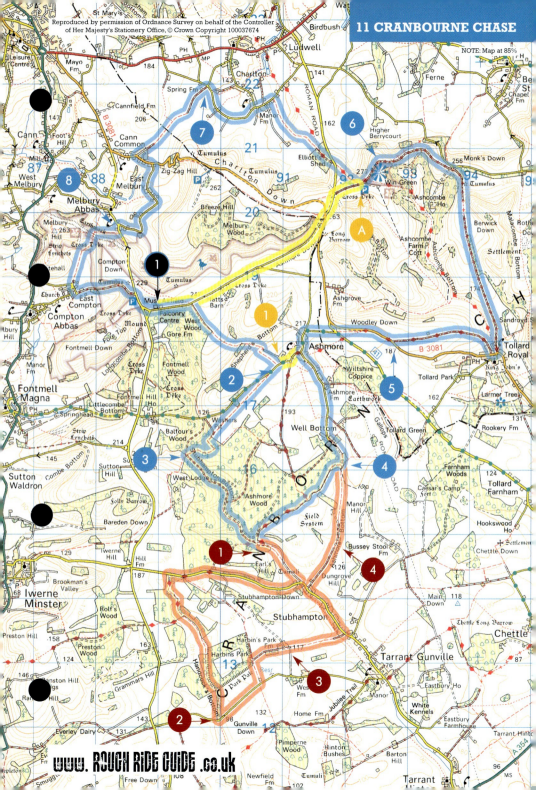

29.6KM (18.4M) 760 metres of climbing

1 **START.** Turn L on the rd for 0.5km (0.3m) then R on a BW (ST 895/186), going along the edge of a wood, DH, to the bottom, then (steep) back UH, turning R by farm entrance, then L to a rd (909/176) and turn R or see shortcut 1.

2 Shortly bear L on a BW, through a gate into a field (as rd starts going DH), DH, into another field and down to the far corner. Enter the woods and bear L to a T-J and turn R, DH, to a X-tracks (895/162).

3 Turn L along Stubhampton Bottom, for 1.85km (1.15m) to a T-J (907/148) and turn L or see the extension. UH on ST, and along the edge of the wood for 2.1km (1.3m), to the bottom and turn L on Well Bottom BW (919/161).

4 Join a rd and keep SA, UH into Ashmore (913/178) and keep R. **4A** As you leave the village turn R on a rd (914/182) (Tollard Royal), to a T-J and go SA on a BW. At the B3081 (923/182) turn R on it for 0.5km (0.3m) then L on a BW (928/180).

5 Follow this DH, getting steep at the end, into Tollard Royal and turn L to a X-rds (944/178). Turn L on the ByW, steep UH at the start, for 3km (1.9m) and keep L (by a minor rd) (937/207) to/past Win Green viewpoint.

6 At start of DH turn R on BW (923/205), steep DH, or see shortcut 2. Over a rd, and keep SA. 1.4km (0.85m), past Elliott's Shed, at a rd (908/218), turn L on it and follow it for 1.45km (0.9m) to a X-rds (898/220) (BW on L).

7 Turn L on the BW and follow this for 1.6km (1m) to the B3081 rd in Cann Common (887/209). Turn L for 0.3km (0.2m), then R on another rd through East Melbury, to a T-J (884/198) and turn L then very shortly R on a BW.

8 UH for 0.4km (0.25m) to a X-tracks (880/197) and turn L on the BW dropping steeply DH and to a rd in East Compton. Keep L on the rd, and L again on a ROW (877/188), steep UH to a rd and turn R on this, then the next L, back to the airfield, (890/185).

EXTENSION
+9.5KM (5.9M) +150 metres climbing

1 Keep SA/R, out of the woods, along a grassy track to the corner of a rd (913/143). Turn R and follow this rd UH for 2.2km (1.35m) to the end of some woods and turn L on a BW (rusty gate). Good ST through the woods, to a rd at the end (900/121).

2 Turn L, UH, for 0.8km (0.5m) then L on a BW (906/127), past a barrier, by a barn. Follow this wide grassy track for 0.3km (0.2m) to the corner of a dirt farm track and turn R on this (905/130). Go past the farm and keep SA on the BW as the drive turns R.

3 Follow this grassy DT, DH to a rd (920/135) and turn L on this. After 1km (0.6m) by the last few houses (Little Pasture), turn R on a gravel DT BW. Go past the farm house, through a gate on to a wide grassy track and along the shallow valley bottom.

4 Go through a gate at the end into the woods and turn L then immediately R (before going UH) on Well Bottom BW and rejoin the main route at no.4.

SHORTCUT 1:
-8KM (5M) -200 metres of climbing

1 Turn L on the rd, into Ashmore and a T-J (913/178). Turn L to and rejoin the main route at no.4.

SHORTCUT 2:
-6.3KM (3.9M) -220 metres of climbing

A Stay on the ByW down to the rd and turn L on this, to a X-rds (917/200). Go SA on the rd opposite and follow this (with great views), back to the airfield (890/185).

GETTING THERE: The ride starts from Compton Abbas airfield, south of Shaftesbury. As you leave Shaftesbury south on the A350, bear East on the A30 then immediately south on the B3081 at Cann Common and follow the signposts to the airfield (890/185). No railway nearby.

ACCOMMODATION: B&B at Sixpenny Handley on 01725 552319 / www.bandbtownfarmbungalow.co.uk, The Old Forge in Compton Abbas on 01747 811881, The Retreat in Shaftesbury on 01747 850372, Camping at Blackmore Vale Park in Shaftesbury on 01747 851523 or in Sixpenny Handley on 01725 552563, Blandford TI on 01258 454770

BIKE SHOPS : Offcamber in Blandford Forum on tel: 01258 458677.

REFRESHMENTS: There is a good cafe at the airfield (sit & watch the planes), a pub in Tollard Royal and a farm tea shop off the extension in Tarrant Gunville.

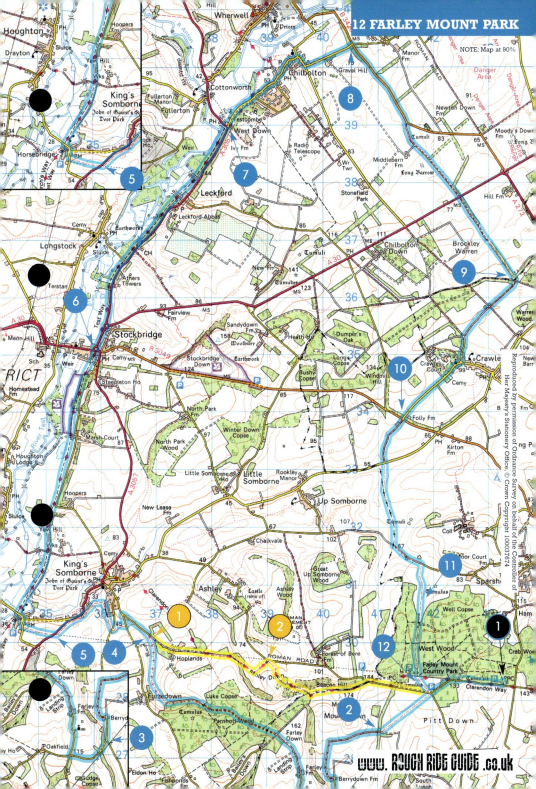

42.2KM (26.2M) 475 metres climbing

1 **START.** At the entrance of the car park turn R on a BW (horseshoe sign) just before and parallel to the rd. This rejoins the rd after 0.6m and you keep SA/R on the rd. After 0.65km (0.4m) at a (rd) T-J (SU 419/291) go SA on a BW (ROW), for 1.2km (0.75m) to a DT (410/284).

2 Turn R on the DT, UH, for 1km (0.6m) to a X-tracks (grassy DT SA and field on R), (401/282) and turn L on a grassy DT. Bear L, then R around a farm and barn, to a T-J with a rd and turn R on this for 0.4km (0.25) to a fork (402/272) and bear R.

3 UH for 0.8km (0.5m) to an off-set X-rds (395/269) and turn R (Farley church, no through rd). Through a farm, UH, for 0.8km (0.5m) to a X-tracks (391/284) and go SA on the DT, into the woods (ST on L avoids the wet DT). Keep SA on this main track for 3.7km (2.3m) to a rd (368/301) and turn L on this or see the shortcut.

4 Turn L on the rd, for 0.65km (0.4m) then turn sharp L (363/304), for 0.25km (0.15m) then R on a BW (364/302). To another rd and go SA on the BW, bearing R (towards houses) for 0.5km (0.3m) and follow the BW as it turns L (360/307). After 1km (0.65m) (parallel to a rd) turn R over the rd, and go SA on the BW (351/301).

5 0.65km (0.4m) to a rd and turn R, down to a fork and bear L (Houghton), over a bridge and turn immediately R on the 'Test way' (345/305). Follow this nice track for 4.8km (3m), joining a drive, to a roundabout (358/350), with the White heart inn on the R, and go SA.

6 0.3km (0.2m) to another roundabout and go SA/L, for 0.65km (0.4m) then turn L at a lay-by, on the 'Test way'. Keep SA on this for 4km (2.5m) then turn R immediately after passing under a brick bridge, to a rd (382/389).

7 Turn L on the rd and keep L for 1.8km (1.1m) (on Coley lane, then L on Village street, past the post office and Abbots mitre pub) to a grass triangle (395/401). Turn R on Winchester street (Newton stacy), which bears L to some X-rds (405/403), and turn R (Winchester).

8 UH for 1.8km (1.1m), then bear R on a BW as the rd bears L (415/390). After 0.4km (0.25m) keep SA/L on a grassy DT, and keep SA on this for 1.2km (0.75m) to a rd. Go SA for 1.8km (1.1m) to a X-tracks (434/362) and take the 2nd R (SA/R), through a silver gate (out of the woods).

9 Keep SA for 1.4km (0.85m), through a gate and turn L (424/353), becoming a rd, to a T-J (425/348) by the church in Crawley. Turn R on the rd for 1.45km (0.9m) to a T-J with the B3049rd and go SA on the BW.

10 0.9km (0.55m) to a rd (411/331) and go SA on the BW, for 1.45km (0.9m) to a DT and turn L on this. After 0.4m, past a barn, turn R on a BW (417/313), and go through a wooden gate into the woods.

11 Keep SA on the DT in the woods, for 1km (0.6m) then keep SA out of the woods, past 3 wooden stumps. As you exit the woods bear L, UH, across the common, to a rd at the top (419/291) and go L on it h (been here before).

12 After 0.5km (0.3m) take the ST (you used before) on the L (425/293), just after a BW (and a DT entrance to the woods), back to the car park (433/292).

SHORTCUT:
-24KM (15M) -165 metres of climbing

1 R on the rd and keep SA between some buildings, becoming the Claren-don Way (C.W.) ByW. This bears R, DH, then L to a rd (390/296) and turn R on the C.W. BW just before the rd.

2 UH on this for 1.1km (0.7m) then turn L on the C.W. BW at the top (397/290) and follow this for 1.1km (0.7m), DH, to a rd. Turn R on this for 1.1km (0.7m) to a fork in the rd (419/291) and turn L (been here before) and rejoin the main route at no 12.

GETTING THERE: This ride starts from (one of the many) Farley Mount Country Park (FMCP) car parks, in the south east corner of West Wood. The car park is just west along a minor road of where Sarum road crosses Sparsholt road, then shortly on the right (433/292). There are also some toilets here and a BBQ and hut for hire.

ACCOMMODATION: B&B in Winchester (nr Sarum rd) on: 01962 861166, B&B in Comton (just south of Winchester) on: 01962 712162, YHA in Winchester on: 0870 7706092. Camping off the B3049 (between Crawley & Sparsholt): 01962 776486, Winchester T.I. on: 01962 840500

BIKE SHOPS: Hargroves Cycles in Winchester, (on Jewry Street) tel: 01962 860005.

REFRESHMENTS There are pubs at Horse-bridge, Stockbridge, The (very good) Mayfly in West Down, Chilbolton and Crawley and a BBQ for hire at the FMCP (tel: 01962 846034).

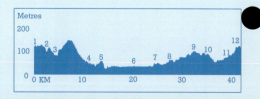

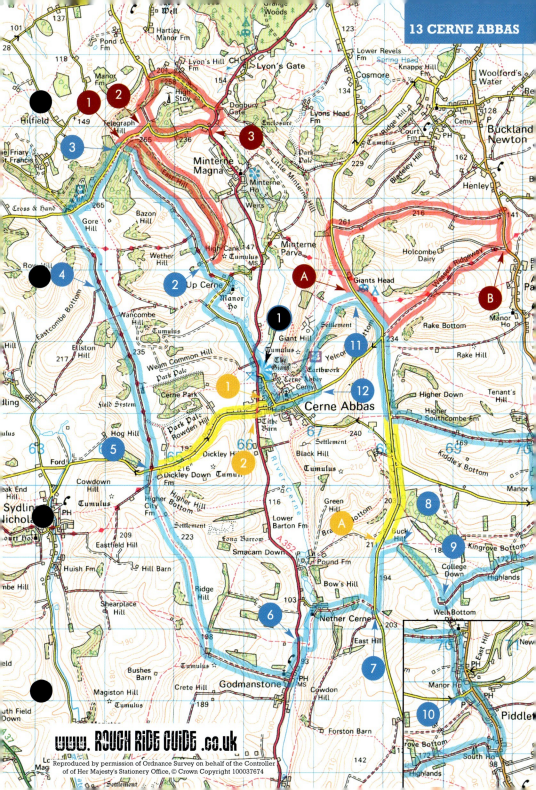

28.7KM (17.8M) 590 metres climbing

1 **START**. Turn R (north) on the A352 or see shortcut 1. for 0.25m (0.15m) then bear L on a rd (ST 661/018) (Up Cerne). Bears R after 0.6m, for another 0.3m to Up Cerne manor house and turn L, on 'No through road' (658/028).

2 0.5km (0.3m) keep SA on a DT as the tarmac rd deteriorates and follow this SA. **2A** After 1.6km (1m) keep SA on a BW, as the DT bears L, steep UH, into the trees, to a rd at the top (642/047) and turn L on this or see extension 1.

3 After 1.2km (.75m), at Gore Hill X-rds (635/038), just past a picnic area, turn L on a stoney BW. Becomes ST, before joining a farm rd, and keep SA/L (south-south-east) for 0.65km (0.4m) to a fork (639/027).

4 Keep SA/L, leaving the main track which bears R, and follow this (Wessex Ridgeway) track, SA. After 2.65km (1.65m), past a big mast, to a rd (647/002), go SA on the BW through Higher City Farm.

5 Cross to the other side of the hedge at Mr Leaf's Dorset gate, heading south. Just after some trees turn L at a BW X-tracks (SY 655/977) DH on rutted DT for 1.3km (0.8m) to the A352 rd at Godmanstone (667/973). Turn L on this rd for 0.55km (0.35m) then turn R on a BW (668/978).

6 DH, over 2 small bridges over the river, then L (669/978) alongside it on a good track. 0.5km (0.3m) to Nether Cerne (670/983) and turn sharp R, steeply UH, keeping L after 0.3km (0.2m), becoming a rougher track, to a wide track/rd at the top (679/983).

7 Go through some gates to the main rd and turn L on this for 0.8km (0.5m) then turn R on a BW, (679/991), or see shortcut 2. After 0.3km (0.2m) turn R through a gate onto a (little used) BW (683/992).

8 Go alongside the hedge, then bear L then R through a gate into the woods, heading south-east, down the valley. Exit the woods (686/987) and go across the field (south-east) past some animal shelters (689/984) and turn L, UH.

9 Follow this concrete track for 2.25km (1.4m), DH, to a rd (708/991) and turn L on this. After 1km (0.6m) (through Piddletrenthide), turn L on another rd (704/999) (Cerne Abbas) for just 0.15km then R on a stoney DT (702/998).

10 Keep SA for 0.9km (0.55m) to a X-tracks (ST 702/006) and turn L on a ByW. UH, for 2.2km (1.35m) to a rd (681/009). Turn R on this rd for 1.85km (1.15m) then L through a gate on a BW (676/026) or see extension 2.

11 0.4km (0.25m) to a fork (673/025) and go L, on Giant Hill, to a BW sign and bear L on a ST, following the fence on the RHS (leaving obvious track bearing R). DH, for 1km (0.65m) and through a gate onto a DT to a rd (670/013).

12 Turn R, for 0.65km (0.4m) into Cerne Abbas and turn R on Duck Street (664/011), by the New Inn pub and follow this for 0.5km (0.3m) back to the car park (662/016).

SHORTCUT 1:
-6.6KM (4.1M) -85 metres of climbing

1 Go south on Duck Street, into Cerne Abbas, to a T-J (ST 664/011) by the New Inn pub and turn R (Dorchester) on Long Street. 0.3km (0.2m) to a X-rds with A352 rd (662/ 010) and go SA on Sydling rd opposite, UH.

2 After 1.85km (1.15m) (before going DH), turn L on a BW (647/ 002) (Higher city farm) and rejoin route at no.5.

EXTENSION 1:
+8.2KM (5.1M) +270 metres climbing

1 Turn R on a BW on the right-hand side of the rd, joining the rd after 0.3km (0.2m), for 0.25km (0.15m) then turn L onto a grassy DT, not the DT SA though, (no signposts), leaving the rd which bears sharp R (ST 646/050).

2 This bears R, DH, becoming a loose, rocky trail to a rd (647/057). Turn R on this rd for 1.1km (0.7m) to a X-rds and turn R (on the A352) for 0.3km (0.2m) then turn R again on another rd (655/050), UH.

3 After 1.3km (0.8m) (past the start of the DH), turn L on a BW (645/049). Bumpy and grassy, but gets better, and steeper DH, for 2.4km (1.5m) to a T-J (654/031). Been here before. Turn R and rejoin the main route at no.2A.

SHORTCUT 2:
-6KM (3.7M) -180 metres of climbing

A Stay on this rd for a further 3.7km (2.3m) (4.5km/2.8m in total) then turn L through a gate on a BW (676/026) and rejoin the main route at no.11.

EXTENSION 2:
+7.1KM (4.4M) +145 metres climbing

A Keep SA on this rd for another 1km (0.65m) then turn R on a DT, BW (ST 673/036). DH on this rocky DT for 2.65km (1.65m) to a rd (697/038) and turn R on this for 0.5km (0.3m) then turn R (698/033) on a DT, to a fork and keep L, UH, on the Wessex Ridgeway.

B 1.4km (0.85m) to a X-tracks (silver gate SA) and bear L, past a barn, then R (effectively SA) on a DT with long grass. UH, for 0.9km (0.55m) to a X-rds (680/021) and turn R for 0.65km (0.4m) then L through a gate on a BW (676/026) and rejoin the main route at no.11.

GETTING THERE: This ride starts in a free carpark, with great views of a Giant on the hillside, with a huge erection. Yes it's Cerne Abbas, a village on the A352 rd, which runs north (from Sherborne - east of Yeovil) to south (Dorchester). Follow the signs for the picnic and viewing point, to a car park at the northern end of the village (662/016) and behold the wonderful sight. Train station at Maiden Newton - follow the Wessex Rideway (NE) for 5km/3m to the route at no5.

ACCOMMODATION: B&B at River Cottage on 01300 341355 and Hazel cottage on 01300 341618, both in Cerne Abbas. Nearest YHA is in Litton Cheyney (east of Dorchester) on 0870 241 2314. Camping at Giant's Head Caravan & Camping Park on 01300 341242. Dorchester T.I. on 01305 267992

BIKE SHOPS: Dorchester Cycles on 01305 268787

Yeovil Cycle Centre on 01935 422000 and P.D.E. Cycles on 01935 72151, both in Yeovil.

REFRESHMENTS: Its only small, but there are 3 pubs in Cerne Abbas, as well as the Singing Kettle tearoom, and a shop. There are also pubs in Godmanstone and Piddletrenthide on the route.

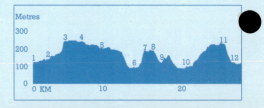

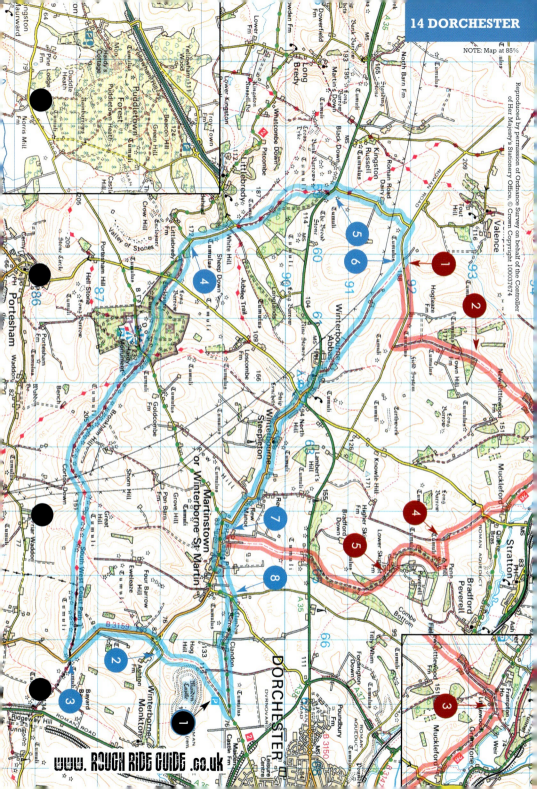

23.8KM (14.8M) 460 metres of climbing

① START. Looking at the castle, go along the track which runs along the right-hand side of the car park. Go along the RHS of a field to a gate and join a second BW with the castle to your left and go DH, **through a field to a rd** (SY 662/881).

② Turn R on the rd, follow the road with a cricket ground to your left, SA at a X-rds, to the B3159 and turn L on this (660/878). UH, **for 1.45km (0.9m)** to the top where a BW crosses the rd and turn R through a gate on (South West Coast Path) BW (662/866).

③ Head west, good, fast BW **for 5.3km (3.3m)** towards the Hardy Monument, **to a rd and go SA into Black Down.** 0.15km at a fork (614/878) **bear L** up a dirt ramp and follow trail for 1.3km (0.8m) to a rd (604/882). Go SA on the BW, which bears L to **join the rd after 0.3m** (600/884).

④ Turn R on the rd, keeping SA at a triangle, to a (rd) T-J (596/892) with 2 BW's SA **and take the R (Jubilee Trail)** BW. Down this gravel path to the edge of a wood and **turn R through a gate** and head over the field, through another gate and the RHS of the field, joining a track **to the rd** (591/907).

⑤ Turn L on the (A35) rd for just 0.15km, then turn R (590/908) on a rd (Compton Valence), UH, **for 1.45km (0.9m)** to T-J (596/920). Turn R on the rd for 0.65km (0.4m) then R on a BW (601/919) or see the *extension*.

⑥ Follow the left-hand side of the field, to a gate, and join a good track, **down to the A35 rd in Winterbourne Abbas** (618/905). Turn L on this rd **for 0.25km (0.15m)** to a fork (621/904) **and bear R** on the B3159 and follow this for **3.2km (2m) into Martinstown.**

⑦ Shortly after the church turn L on the Clandon BW (648/899), **and shortly up here, turn R through a metal gate on the BW** (649/890) 0.5km (0.3m) to a rd (654/891) and **go SA on a the BW**, through Clandon **and keep SA to a rd** (672/891) and turn R on this, back to the car park (672/891).

•**NOTE:** Puddletown Forest (shown in the extra map) is just north east of Dorchester (off the A35 rd), and has some nice trails in it, and is well worth exploring.

EXTENSION:
+6.3KM (3.9M) 145 metres of climbing

① Continue along the rd for a further 1.45km (0.9m) (2.1km/1.3m in total) then turn L signposted to Town Hill Farm (614/918). Follow the rd for 1.1km (0.7m), past the farm buildings and into woods, **after 0.3km (0.2m), keep SA as you exit the woods,** DH on a BW (616/931).

② Follow this BW, **for 1.95km (1.2m)**, joining a better track, alongside stream, to a T-J with a rd (628/944). Turn R (Frampton) for 0.3km (0.2m) then turn R then immediately L, following the National Cycle Network #26, **on a tarmac BW** (631/945).

③ Follow this for 1.3km (0.8m) until you see a cottage to the left and stables to the right (639/936) and **bear R, past the stables.** 0.5km (0.3m) to a rd (640/932) and go SA, UH, on a gravel track **for 0.8km (0.5m).** Just as you pass a small clump of trees, **turn L through the hedges,** onto a BW (644/925).

④ Steep UH for **0.3km (0.2m), through a silver gate** as the hill levels, **then turn R through another gate** into the trees (648/926). Go along the gravel track through the trees, then as you emerge, **bear L** (646/918) past the farm buildings, to T-J with a gravel rd, back into some woods.

⑤ Turn R on the gravel track for 1.6km (1m) to the A35 rd (647/904) and go SA (slightly R) on the (Martinstown) BW. Follow this **for a 1.45km (0.9m)** grassy DH to the B3159 rd in Martinstown (645/890) and turn L for 0.3km (0.2m) and rejoin the main route at no.7.

GETTING THERE: The ride starts from the Maiden Castle carpark, which is just south-west of Dorchester (which is north of Weymouth). At the roundabout with the A354, on the southern side of Dorchester, go north on the B3147 (past Tesco), and turn left following the signs to for the 'Maiden Castle Road' to Maiden Castle carpark (668/889). Train station in Dorchester.

ACCOMMODATION: B&B in Winterbourne Abbas (west of Dorchester) on 01305 889296, B&B in Weymouth on 01305 785408 Hotel in Dorchester on 01305 264043 YHA on Litton Cheyney (east of Dorchester) on 0870 241 2314 Camping at Bagwell Farm Touring Park, in Chickerell on 01305 782 575 Dorchester T.I. on 01305 267992

BIKE SHOPS : Dorchester Cycles on 01305 268787, Weymouth Cycle Centre on 01305 835 907

REFRESHMENTS: Tesco's (with a cafe) in southern Dorchester (on the B3147), and pubs in Winterbourne Abbas and Martinstown on the return leg. There is nothing more on the extension.

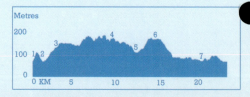

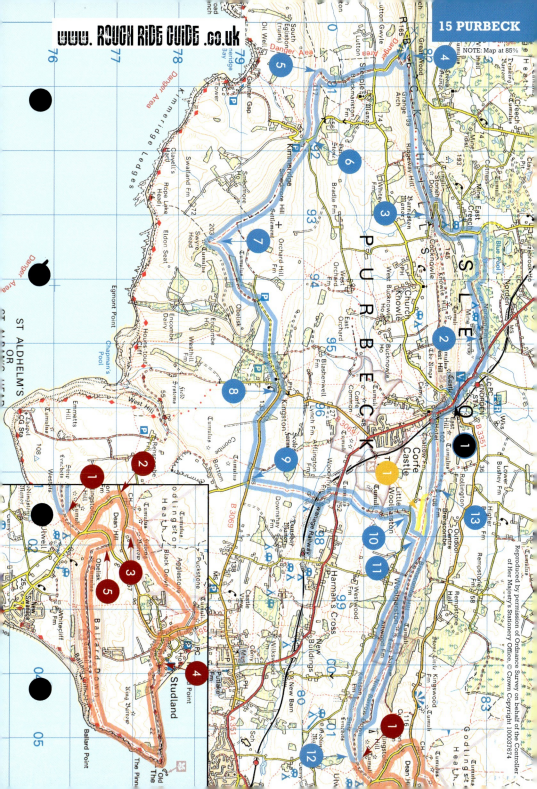

29.5KM (18.3M) 820 metres of climbing

① START. Turn R (north-west) on the A351, SA at the roundabout (Wareham) for 0.3km (0.2m) then L to Norden Farm (SY 952/829). Go past the campsite reception, SA to the caravan site and to the far R corner of the field to a BW, into the woods (947/829).

② Follow this BW (and occasional signs to East Creech) for 1.6km (1m) to a rd (933/829). Turn L on this rd, and keep SA (south) as it turns R, past a chalky embankment, then hairpins UH. At the top (after 1.45km/0.9m) turn R on the Ridgeway Hill & Tyneham BW (931/821).

③ Go through the wooden gate onto the gravel BW, keeping the fence to your L. 0.8km (0.5m) to a X-tracks (922/ 819) (farm track R and grassy DH L) and go through the gate to your L. Continue on the grassy BW (still headed generally W), now with the fence to your R, SA for 1.8km (1.1m) to a car park (at a viewpoint) (905/817).

④ Turn L (Steeple), DH on a steep gravel track for 0.2m to a rd. Turn L on this, DH, for 0.5km (0.3m) to a X-rds (907 /812) (where the rd turns L) and go SA on the gravel track (Steeple Leaze Farm). Past a farmhouse and campsite, into the trees, UH, on a rough track, bearing R, and ending at a rusty metal gate (908/803).

⑤ Go through this into and around the LHS of the field, east to the far corner and a silver metal gate after 0.3km (0.2m). Go through the gate, and head east on a grassy track with a fence to the R, for 1.1km (0.7m) to a rd (918/801).

⑥ Turn R to a T-J, and turn L then R (effectively SA) on a gravel BW and follow this for 2.4km (1.5m) (steep drop and view of the sea R), to a large tumulus at Swyre Head (934/785) (just ahead is a bench with great views). Turn L almost back on yourself, following the sign for Kingston.

⑦ 1.45km (0.9m) to a car park (943/793), and turn R on the narrow tarmac rd, UH. Keep SA to a T-J (957/796) with the B3069 rd (Scott Arms Hotel L).

⑧ Go R on the 'B' rd (Swanage) for 1.6km (1m) then L through a metal gate on a BW (Wooyhynde & Little Woolgarston), opposite a rd to Worth Matravers, (972/791).

⑨ 1.6km (1m), DH, under railway, past Woody Hyde farm to the A351 rd (973/805). Cross the rd to go SA through 2 silver metal gates on the (Woolgarston) BW. Follow the grassy track, becoming tarmac, past farm buildings, to a T-J with a narrow rd (after 1.3km/0.8m) (976/817).

⑩ Turn R, UH on the rd for 0.3km (0.2m) to the top and turn L on (Brenscombe Hill) BW (980/817). Grassy UH, for 0.15km (0.1m) to a gate (980/819) and go through this and turn R or see the shortcut.

⑪ Turn R and follow this (SP to Ulwell), along the hillside and keep SA over a couple of X-tracks (after 0.5km/0.3m, and 2.75km/1.7m) heading east along the hillside, for 3.7km (2.3m) to a wider track going steeply DH (SZ 013/808) and turn sharp L on this, UH, or see the extension.

⑫ To the top (008/811) and bear L along the field edge, and keep SA on the obvious track, along the hill top. Follow this along the hilltop for 3.8km (2.35m) to a mast (SY 973/822) and bear L at the fork on the ST DH (west).

⑬ 0.9km (0.55m) to a rd and go R on this, under the railway to a T-J (961/822) with the A351 rd. Go R on this for 0.4km (0.25m) then R back to the car park (959/825).

SHORTCUT:
-7.4KM (4.6M) -200 metres of climbing

① Turn L along the hillside for 0.65km (0.4m) to a X-tracks (SY 974/820) and turn R, UH, towards the tall mast, then shortly L on a ST BW (972/822) (nr the mast) and rejoin the main route at no 12.

EXTENSION:
+12KM (7.5M) & +415 metres climbing

① Keep SA/R on this broader track, DH, keeping L at a round hill, SA, to a rd (after 0.5km/0.3m) (018/812). Turn L on the rd then immediately keep L at the fork, UH, for 0.8km (0.5m) to a T-J (012/818) with the B3351 rd.

② Turn R on the B rd (past the golf club) for 0.5km (0.3m) then L on a BW through a small gate at a little parking area (017/819). Keep SA for 0.25km (0.15m) past open part of the golf course to a fork (018/821) and bear R.

③ Follow the BW DH for 1.6km (1m) to a track (030/829) and turn R to the B3351. Go R on this, for 0.4km (0.25m) into Studland and turn L on School Lane (034/825) by Studland Stores. Go to the end of this rd, by the toilets, and continue on the BW (Handfast Point).

④ Follow this BW around the coast, on the cliff edge, to a fork (048/815) (after 2.6km/1.6m) and bear R, UH, on Ballard Down BW. Follow this (west) along the ridge to an obelisk (022/813). Go through the gate, bearing R, DH, to the rd (020/816).

⑤ Turn L on this rd, 0.65km (for 0.4m) then turn R on the BW you came down earlier (018/812) (just after a rd on the R). UH, for 0.5km (0.3m) to a fork (014/809) and bear L, UH, on a track you haven't been on and rejoin the main route at no.11.

GETTING THERE: This ride starts from the Corfe Castle car park (south of Poole/Bournemouth) on the Isle of Purbeck (which isn't actually an island, but a penisula). Go through Wareham (west of Poole) then south-east on the A351 (Corfe) for 5 miles and use the Corfe Castle visitor centre car park (959/825). By train: Get a train to Bournemouth then a ferry (regular & cheap) from North Haven Point (037/871) to South Haven Point (join the ride in Studland).

ACCOMMODATION: B&B in Corfe on 01929 480 374. B&B in Church Knowle on 480712. Campsites at Burnbake on 01929 480570 in Rempstone, Ulwell on 422823, Norden farm on 480098 & Bucknowle farm on 480280. YHA in Swanage on 0870 7706058. Swanage T.I. on 01929 422885.

BIKE SHOPS: Bikelab on 01202 330011, and Action Bikes on 680123 both in Poole. Xtreme in Bournemouth on 01202 741744 and Bikeabout in Swanage on 01929 425050.

REFRESHMENTS: A National Trust cafe in the castle entrance, and a choice of pubs & shops in Corfe, and the Scott Arms Hotel in Kingston.

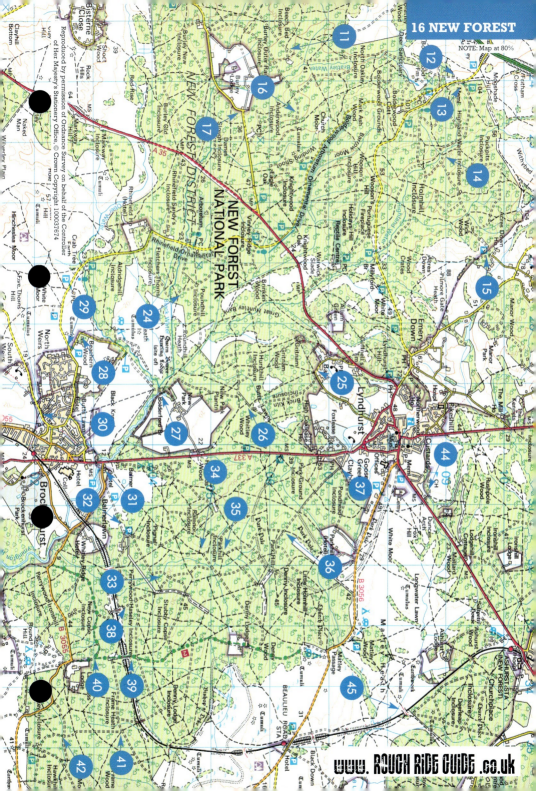

DIY ROUTE

The broad tracks around the forest are all very similar, so rather than trying to follow a set route, just ride as much or as little as you like (see right for ideas of places to visit), and use the numbered markers to orientate yourself.

THE HISTORY

William the Conqueror made this area a royal hunting ground in 1079 when he discovered it's beauty (and the many deer that lived there). He couldn't have been a very good hunter though, as there are lots of deer still living here, as well as over 5,000 ponies and cattle which roam wild on 45,000 acres of open forest. This has been a right for many of the locals, and as many 400 (commoners) excercise the right to graze their stock.

■ NOTE: Please don't feed the animals as it encourages to stray on to roads. Also, they have plenty of natural food in the forest and they can become quite aggressive.

THE RULES OF THE FOREST

1. Keep to waymarked gravel tracks when cycling.
2. Think ahead and be aware of animals, other cyclists, pedestrians and drivers whether.
3. Always ride in a single file when roads are narrow and never ride more than two abreast.
4. Keep your speed down, give way to walkers and be friendly to ther road users.
5. Make sure you are visable by wearing bright clothing.
6. Always use your lights in the dark or in poor visibility.
7. Keep well away from any work going on in the forest.
8. Don't pass vehicles loading timber until you have been told it is safe to do so.
9. Plan your route to be out of the forest by dusk.

■ NOTE: Because fire is a great threat to the forest no campfires are allowed. There are barbecue sites provided by the Forestry Commission (023 8028 3141).

Also see www.forestry.gov.uk/newforest for more info.

This ancient woodland is mainly made up of old oak and beech trees, and has a wonderful peacefulness about it, as well as a timeless character. There is a 40 mph speed limit for cars on unfenced roads to protect the wildlife (and cyclists). There are also lots of car parks, so please use one of them and take any valuables with you. Obviously there is no driving allowed on the forest tracks.

THE TOWNS & VILLAGES

BEAULIEU (south east)
A lovely village which has National Motor Museum, Palace House, and a 13th Century Abbey to visit, and a pub.

BROCKENHURST (south)
A lovely village where the ponies can often be seen grazing on the village green. There is a 1,000 year old yew tree in the churchyard and at the west end of the main shopping street (Brookley Road) is a wide ford, known as the water splash. Good selection of shops, pubs, etc.

BURLEY (south west)
A pictureque village with cattle often wandering around it. There are also a few tea shops and art galleries and a pick your own farm. It is also famous for its smuggling history and witches.

LYNDHURST (central)
This is the 'Capital' of the forest, and is home to the New Forest Museum and Visitor information centre. There is a good car park and a selection of shops, tea rooms and cafes, etc.

FRITHAM (north)
A small village, home to the famous Royal Oak Inn where smugglers were believed to have gathered years ago.

■ NOTE: There is a New Forest open-top bus which calls at Lyndhurst, Beaulieu, Brockenhurst, and Lymington (on the Isle of Wight) and it has room for your bicycle.

A network of on and off-road cycle routes has been created to link the main villages and railway station at Brockenhurst. You may walk on any footpath or track, unless it says otherwise, but cyclists must keep to the main gravel surfaced forest tracks.

OTHER PLACES WORTH VISITING:
Purpose built MTB trails (aimed at kids), see www.avontyrrell.org.uk
Burley Deer Park
Longdown activity farm (Totton)
Marwell Zoological Park (Colden Common)
Otter and Wildlife park, near Ashurst
Paultons Leisure Park in Ower (just off exit 2 of the M27)

GETTING THERE: The New Forest is south-west of Southampton. From the M27 (junction 1), go south on the A337 (Lyndhurst). There are lots of free car parks all over the forest and in the centre of Lyndhurst village. Train station in Brockenhurst.

ACCOMMODATION: B&B in Brockenhurst on 01590 623707, 622276, and in Burley on 01425 403448 and many more. YHA in Burley on 0870 7705734. There are numerous campsites all over the forest; call 0131 3146505 for more information and bookings at one of the Forestry Commission campsites. New Forest T.I. on 01703 282269.

BIKE SHOPS : Cyclexperience in Brockenhurst on 01590 624204 and in Christchurch on 01202 486278 (also do bike hire). Forest Leisure Cycling in Burley on 01425 403584 and in Beaulieu on 01590 611029 (also do bike hire).

REFRESHMENTS: There are lots of pubs around the forest, but if you don't bump into any by chance, head to a village which will most likely have a pub, shop and usually a tea room or two.

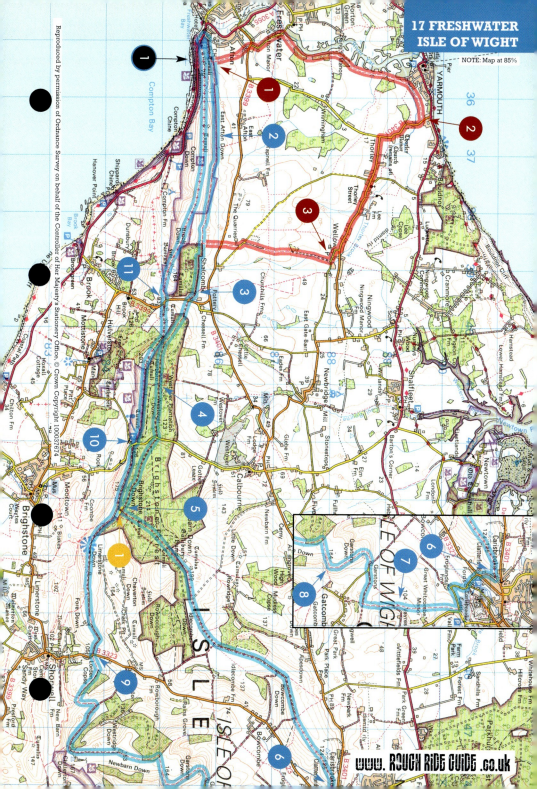

37KM (23M) 870 metres of climbing

1 START. Go towards Freshwater on the A3055 rd, after 0.15km turn R on Southdown rd (SZ 349/857), and shortly R again on the Old Highway, Carisbrooke BW towards the Golf club. 0.7km (0.45m) to a fork and bear L, DH on the (F32 Freshwater way) BW, then shortly R on the Pilgrims way, along the edge of the golf course or see *extension*.

2 After 1.3km (0.8m), at the end of the golf course, go through some gates onto a grassy track, along the bottom, (east). After 2.2km (1.35m), go through a gate, and bear R into the woods (386/857).

3 Follow this BW to a T-J and turn R on the farm track, DH, to the rd (395/855). Cross the rd onto the (Bridgestone forest) BW SA, for 0.5km (0.3m) through a gate, and R at the fork, UH, for 0.65km (0.4m) to a DT (403/851), and turn L on this, for 0.7km (0.45m) to multiple X-tracks.

4 Keep SA on the main track, DH, for 1km (0.6m) to a rd (419/849) and keep SA on the BW. Keep SA at X-tracks on the (BS9 Carisbrooke) BW, keeping R, on the lower track, for 1.45km (0.9m), to Bridgestone down five lane ends (432/ 843) and turn L on the Tennyson trail (N139) or see the *shortcut*.

5 Keep SA on this ByW (SA at some X-tracks, through a gate on the N136a, bearing R on the main track Old Highway N128 Carisbrooke, and SA at the X-tracks on the N123) for 4.2m, DH to a tarmac T-J (481/881).

6 Turn sharp R to the rd and go SA (R then L) at the off-set X-rds onto Clatterford Shute (481/877). After 0.65km (0.4m), through 2 fords, bear L at Froglands triangle (483/872). After 0.4km (0.25m) (castle on L) turn R on the (Gatcombe N108) BW (486/874), before Whitcombe rd.

7 1km (0.65m) to a fork and bear L on (Gatcombe G6) BW (486/863), 0.65km (0.4m) to a X-tracks (486/ 857). Turn R, for 0.8km (0.5m) then turn L on the (Downs, Shorwell) BW, just past a house on the R (478/858). Around a chalk pit, steep UH, through a gate, and keep SA around the side of the hill for 0.8km (0.5m) to a tree (478/850).

8 Turn R at the tree, through a gate to a T-J in the woods (474/849) and turn L, to a barn. After 1.6km (1m) bear R by the radar mast and keep R at the X-tracks onto a concrete rd (474/834). After 1km (0.6m) turn L on BW (blue arrow) (466/ 838), to gate and keep R through more gates and R along edge of woods, DH to a rd (457/838).

9 Go SA on the (SW51 Freshwater) BW, and keep SA for 2km (1.25m) (surface changes) to the viewpoint at top of Limerstone down (438/837). Keep SA on the main (BS10 Tennyson trail, Lynch lane) track, through some gates, keeping the wood on the RHS, for 1.95km (1.2m) to a rd.

10 Turn R on the rd, for 0.1km then L through a car park (420/845), on a ByW (Mottistone Down, Freshwater). After 2.1km (1.3m) keep SA at some X-tracks with a dirt road, through a gate into a field (402/850) and bear L on the DT, through fields, for 0.65km (0.4m) to a rd (395/850).

11 Go SA on the track opposite, turning L at the bottom of the chalk pit, to some gates and bear R at the fork, UH on a chalk track. Follow this ByW for 4.5km (2.8m) along the ridge top (Brook Down), through a golf course, to a fork (359/ 857). Go L/SA on the (Tennyson Trail, old highway) ByW, to the A3055 rd and L back to the start (351/856).

EXTENSION:
+7.25KM (4.5M) 45 metres of climbing

1 Stay on the (Freshwater) F32 BW, for 0.65km (0.4m), DH to a rd and bear R on this to the main B3399 rd (350/865). Go SA/L on the (Causeway) rd, for 0.7km (0.45m), then turn R on a (cycle path) BW (348/871). Follow this for 3.2km (2m) along the riverside, bearing to the R of Yarmouth, to the B3401 rd (364/896).

2 Turn R on this rd, staying L on this after 0.9km (0.55m) (366/888), through Thorley village. After another 2.2km (1.35m), turn R, in Wellow village, on the round island cycle route (386/881), for 0.25km (0.15m) then turn R on the (S19 Hamstead Trail) BW, (388/880), by the brook.

3 UH for 1.6km (1m) to a rd (by a thatched cottage) and turn L then immediately R on a driveway (The Quarries) (385/863). Keep SA on the BW, to the B3399 rd and go SA on the BW opposite, UH for 0.4km (0.25m), to a X-tracks (386/857) and turn L, and rejoin route at No.3.

SHORTCUT:
-18.8KM (11.7) -375 metres of climbing

1 Turn R at the X-tracks, to another X-tracks (FP only SA) and turn R on a DT ByW , and follow this for 1.2km (0.75m) to a rd (421/845), and rejoin the main route at no.10.

GETTING THERE: Get a ferry to the Isle of Wight (WightLink ferries on: 0870 582 0202, www.wightlink.co.uk or Hovertravel on: 01983 811000www.hover-travel.co.uk) and aim for Freshwater. Park in the cliff side car park (351/856), off the A3055. Alternatively, save money and go as a foot passenger from Lymington to Yarmouth and join the ride on the extension.

ACCOMMODATION: B&B in Freshwater on: 01983 753723, B&B's in Carisbrooke on: 01983 524359 /522173 and 523463. Palmerston Hotel on: 01983 865547, Campsites at Grange farm, Brighstone on: 01983 740296, Stoats farm, Totland bay on: 01983 755258 & Compton farm on: 01983 740215, YHA in Totland Bay (on the West coast) on: 0870 7706070, Yarmouth T.I. on: 01983 813818

BIKE SHOPS: First gear on: 01983 521417 and Wight mountain on: 520530 in Newport and Isle cycle hire in Yarmouth on: 01983 760219.

REFRESHMENTS: There aren't any pubs actually on the route, but there are some just off them in: Freshwater, Yarmouth, Carisbrooke, and Shorwell.

bike magic.com

share your **best rides** with the **bikemagic.com** community, upload your **photos** to the **gallery**

Forums **Gear**News **Galleries** **Member**Reviews

rough ride guide presents.....

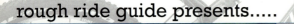

an introduction to mountain biking

buying a bike, setting it up, woman specific bikes, equipment & clothing, winter & night riding, aches & pains, fitness training, suspension, and riding skills, from pedalling to jumping and endo-turns.

Everything you need to know and do to become a better rider

available at www.roughrideguide.co.uk

rough ride guide presents.....

route expansion packs

All of our books have an optional expansion route pack, whether you want more rides for your local area, or some for a totally new area to add to your book

More great routes, at a great price

available at www.roughrideguide.co.uk

NOTE: The Forestry Commission provide hundreds of miles of way marked cycling trails for riders of all abilities. Many of their sites also have activities for the whole family, so they make an excellent location for family trips - see www.forestry.gov.uk for more information.

rough ride guide presents.....

Pictures provided by the Forestry Commission and Andy McCandlish.

man-made trails

Hundreds of way-marked, man-made trails in over 70 destinations in England, Scotland & Wales, providing thousands of miles of trails.

Also includes information on long distance / epic rides

available at www.roughrideguide.co.uk

rough ride guide presents.....

the maintenance & repair manual

Over 100 pages of step-by-step instructions with full colour pictures, for just about every job you are ever likely to do, from cleaning to changing the bottom bracket. This manual can also be updated as and when new components come out.

Saves you time & money

available at www.roughrideguide.co.uk

Stonehenge Cycles

01722 334915

86 Fisherton St. Salisbury, SP2 7QY

Giant
Marin
Kona
Whyte
Specialized

www.stonehengecycles.com

Stonehenge Cycles
Ride the experience

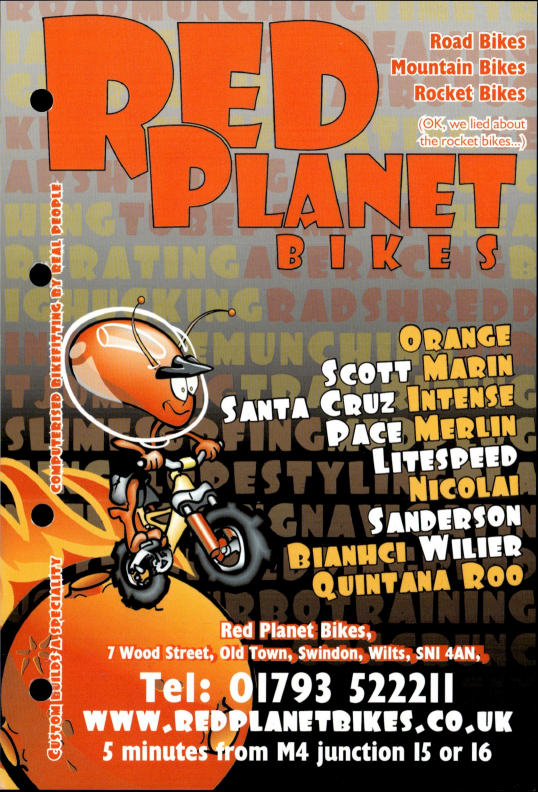

Queens Avenue, Clifton
Bristol, BS8 1SB
Tel: 0117 9293500

79 Station Road
Taunton, TA1 1PB
Tel: 01823 275822

* Massive range of mountain, hybrid and road race bikes and accessories
* Full service, and repair facilities with Cyctech level 3 qualified mechanics
* Lifetime service package FREE when you buy a new bike
* Lowest prices in the UK - we will beat any price

*not in conjunction with any other offer

IMBA - UK
working for mountain biking

Want to support UK trails? Then why not join IMBA!

IMBA-UK supports mountain biking in the UK, and defends rights of way for MTBs. We work to keep trails and public access open by:
* supporting volunteer trail work
* cooperating with trail user groups, land managers and public bodies
* encouraging responsible riding.

Join up at www.imba.org.uk to support UK mountain biking.

www.imba.org.uk
info@imba.org.uk

SPEAK   BUILD   RESPECT   RIDE

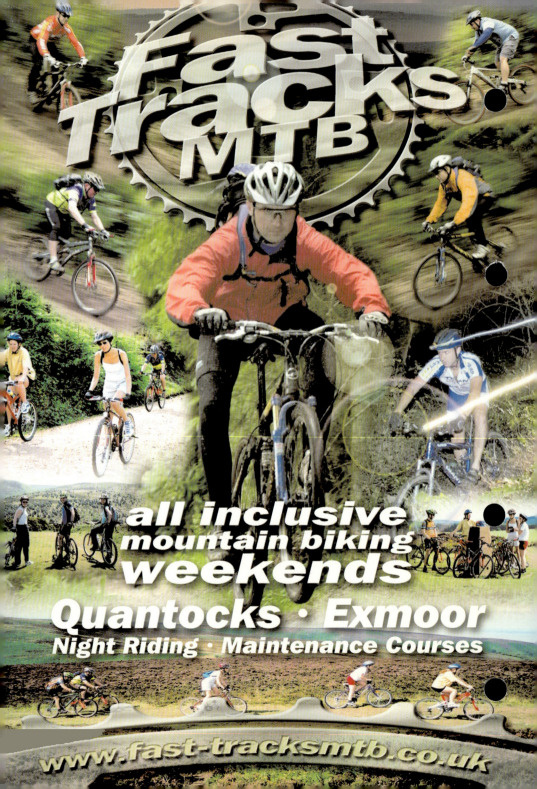

brought to you

by

ROUGH RIDE GUIDE